PRAISE FOR

The Nomadic Soul

"Seline Shenoy's concept of the higher self as a Nomadic Soul is a lyrical, thought-provoking metaphor that leads the reader into self-exploration. In *The Nomadic Soul*, Shenoy offers lucid advice for balancing the tension between our need for freedom and our need for connection, helping us each create our own path through a complicated world."

Martha Beck, PhD, Harvard-trained sociologist, world-renowned coach, and *New York Times* bestselling author

"Seline Shenoy is a true seeker and a deep listener—a true companion. This book is a necessary antidote to the shallowness and lack of purpose that plague our modern lives."

Mark Nepo, *New York Times* bestselling author of *The Book of Awakening*

"Emotionally resonant and brimming with wisdom, *The Nomadic Soul* is a unique roadmap for those of us who long for a more meaningful life. Seline Shenoy takes readers on a profound journey of self-discovery grounded in the stories of those who have walked the path before them and reveals a powerful new way to think about freedom and connection in today's world. This book is a must-read for searchers and seekers looking for greater fulfillment and purpose!"

Stephen Cope, bestselling author of *The Great Work of Your Life*; founder and former director of the Kripalu Institute for Extraordinary Living

"In *The Nomadic Soul*, Seline Shenoy thoughtfully guides readers through an innovative and actionable framework for adding connection, adventure, and discovery to their lives while shining a light on six examples of inspirational individuals who took hold of their visions and mastered their lives. This book is a powerful blueprint for embracing your deepest truth while celebrating the human spirit and staying grounded in your authenticity."

Dondi Dahlin, award-winning author of *The Five Elements* and coauthor of *The Little Book of Energy Medicine*

"Seline Shenoy has written an incredibly insightful, wise, and page-turning classic, reminding us all that the real purpose of life is to explore, uncover, and discover the profound meaning within it just like ancient—and modern—nomads did. *The Nomadic Soul* reminds us that the eternal path to inner peace, happiness, and success is by digging inward, going on our own hero's journeys to be transformed into our true selves, and being content with what we find. In an era that screams that we don't matter unless we acquire certain consumer products, attend certain schools, fabricate a certain online presence, or live a certain type of socially approved but ultimately unfulfilling life, this book stands in stark contrast to the greatest threat facing America—and humanity—today: the poisonous and false idea that our authentic selves are not good enough."

Dr. Rob Carpenter, UCLA faculty member, bestselling author of *The 48 Laws of Happiness*, and Hollywood producer

www.amplifypublishinggroup.com

The Nomadic Soul: A Seeker's Guide to Finding a Sense of Self and Belonging in the Modern World

For more information, please contact:
Amplify Publishing, an imprint of Amplify Publishing Group
620 Herndon Parkway, Suite 220
Herndon, VA 20170
info@amplifypublishing.com

Library of Congress Control Number: 2024904992

CPSIA Code: PRV0424A

ISBN-13: 979-8-89138-219-0

Printed in the United States

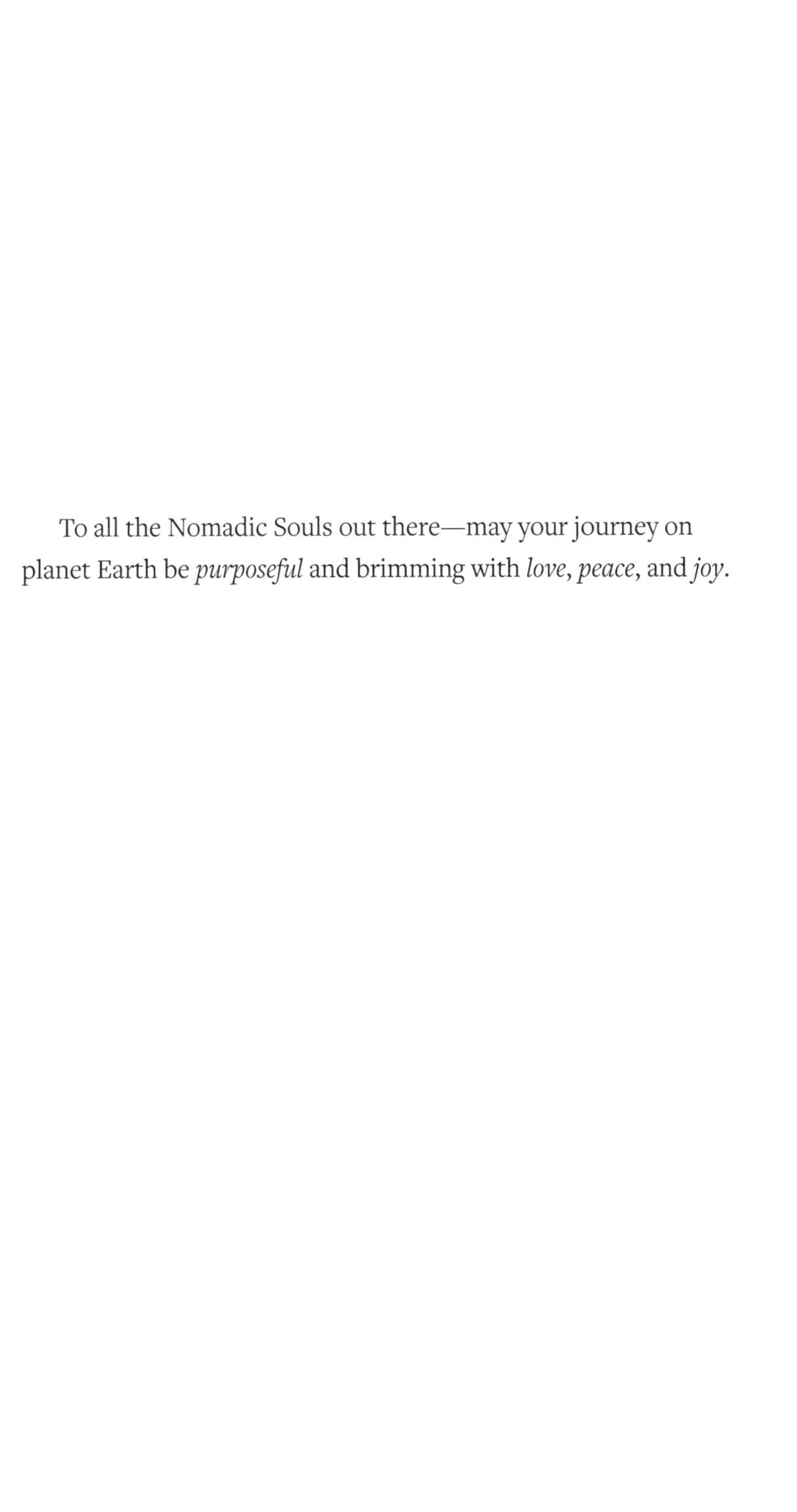

To all the Nomadic Souls out there—may your journey on planet Earth be *purposeful* and brimming with *love*, *peace*, and *joy*.

The Nomadic Soul

A Seeker's Guide to Finding a Sense of Self and Belonging in the Modern World

Seline Shenoy

Contents

Part 2: Connection 151

Preface

"Not all those who wander are lost." — J.R.R. Tolkien

The desert is one of the most challenging places on Earth for a human being to live. The sweltering heat during the day and ice-cold temperatures at night. The absence of food, water, shelter, and people for miles. All of this could spell disaster for any traveler.

Yet these conditions did not deter the ancient desert nomads from traversing hundreds of miles across vast stretches of cascading dunes. They were seeking green pastures, not just for physical sustenance but for the sustenance of their souls. The promise of deep nourishment fueled their will and galvanized their efforts to carry on.

Mounted on top of their camels, dressed in regal, long white tunics with colorful headcloths, these nomads carried with them provisions—supplies of milk, meat, and water.

These days, most of us cannot imagine voyaging through such a hostile environment without using any navigational instrument—such as a simple compass and paper map or our more modern technology like GPS and Google Earth. But not having these tools did not dissuade the desert nomads from venturing forth. They had faith in their sensory faculties and inner knowing.

The nomads mapped out their travels using key landmarks in their natural environments, such as mountains, oases, trees, big rocks, and sand dunes shaped by winds. They could even infer directions by looking up at the sky and observing the patterns and cycles of celestial bodies such as the sun, moon, and star constellations. They considered the sky to be a divine navigational tool that was created to guide humans on their quests. The desert nomads' navigational abilities, combined with their adaptability and resilience, allowed them to thrive in those perilous frontiers.

After many years of traveling these paths, they accumulated sufficient knowledge to get around and adapt to the harsh conditions. They developed their instincts so they could find their way back to safety if they got lost. Their wisdom and expertise were well-preserved and passed down to future generations to continue the legacy of nomadic living.

Although their mental toughness and resourcefulness are admirable, one can't help but wonder: Why would they choose to live in such difficult conditions? Surely there were less life-threatening living arrangements to be found in the villages and towns nearby, where food, water, warmth, and shelter were readily available.

Why not opt for living in a secure settlement instead of being constantly on the move in the desert, exposed to its unpredictable forces and dangers? The standard explanation is that they traveled in search of food, water, and places to grow crops and raise animals.

While that's true, it goes much deeper than that. Living their nomadic ways was an expression of their soul. They found purpose on their odysseys, no matter how foreboding the road ahead seemed. These excursions gave them opportunities to forge deeper bonds with their travel partners, the natural world, the cosmos, and, most importantly, themselves.

In these desolate lands, they were liberated from the cultural labels, roles, and anything else limiting their identity. The vast expanse of cascading dunes offered a refuge in which they could break free from these social conventions and expectations, allowing the nomads to connect with their true essence. In this serene space, the nomads could understand their place in the grander scheme of things.

They were seekers, explorers, and vagabonds, driven by a burning desire to wander off into the wide blue yonder—because in doing so, they uncovered new domains not just around them but within them.

And this primal yearning to be more, do more, and have more lives within you too.

Adopting the ways of the ancient desert nomads can help us break out of the ruts we find ourselves in—whether that's an unfulfilling career, a lackluster relationship, or a general lack of meaning in our lives. All we need to do is look beyond the walls we've built that contain us and indulge our spiritual wanderlust, just as they did.

The nomads show us what's possible when we call forth our courage and faith to step out into uncharted territories. We live up to our potential when we take healthy risks, try new things, say "yes" to the right opportunities, and express our ideas without fear of ridicule.

By granting yourself the freedom to roam free—mind, heart, and soul—you'll find peace, and the solutions to your most vexing problems will appear in unexpected places. All you need to do is believe. Believe that you have the power to take that journey—just as ancient nomads did.

The Nomadic Soul and Its Core Needs

The desert nomads' impulse to roam the open desert, under the luminous sun and starry, moonlit sky, was perhaps the earliest and purest expression of the Nomadic Soul—a deeper, ethereal aspect of our identity that dwells within us all and holds the key to everything from life's biggest question to the minutiae of everyday existence.

Nomads, by definition, are people who do not stay long in the same place. They're known to roam from one place to the next without the real intent to transform into a better version of themselves. At first glance, they appear as lost and restless souls devoid of an anchor or stability. This is *not* the way of the Nomadic Soul modeled by ancient desert nomads. Rather, a person who embodies the Nomadic Soul is someone who journeys with purpose. They do it to transform, gain wisdom, and benefit those around them. They embark on a sacred quest in search of meaning, truth, and purpose. The journey of the Nomadic Soul is an investigation of a different plane where they traverse deeper dimensions of existence.

Movement is the central theme of some of the most beloved novels and literary works. Books like *The Alchemist* by Paulo Coelho, *Eat, Pray, Love* by Elizabeth Gilbert, and *Siddhartha* by Hermann Hesse speak to a primal part of us, a longing to unearth our hidden layers. Even our greatest religious stories, from Confucius to Moses, talk about the journey of discovery being a vital rite of passage in our spiritual evolution. Going on sacred trips to attain enlightenment is a practice that dates back to prehistoric times, when shamans and holy men left their clans to embark on their own journey. They went on perilous journeys to destinations of great cultural and spiritual importance. These rigorous acts of sacrifice were about much more than just reaching a specific destination. They offered travelers a chance to reflect, focus inward, and discover new destinations within themselves.

On some level, our entire lives are a holy quest—a journey in search of self, which may or may not involve physical movement. During pivotal moments in our lives, we'll feel the urge to move from a knowingness—an old identity that we used to feel at home with—toward new territory. This is because the soul has a particular trajectory of evolution. It wants to transition to another place because we're no longer satisfied with the old. It's up to us to heed the call to transform. We feel it instinctually when we're stuck in a situation that does not feel right for us anymore or when we know we can accomplish so much more. Cartoonist Charles M. Schulz captured this angst when he said, "There is no greater burden than great potential."

As travelers, what's important is that we stay with ourselves in the process and go as far inward as we can. That's where we'll find the answers we seek and hear the whispers of our hearts. We can't find those on the surface of life. We have to drill down to our core foundation. If we want to find water in our backyard, we don't dig up small holes all over the yard. Instead, we find one spot and dig as deep as we can. Eventually, water will spring forth from that opening. The plentitude a Nomadic Soul seeks is found with the same attention, care, and willingness to travel inward to the substratum of our being.

Nomadic Souls in the Modern Age

Being nomadic is not a new concept. We have always been a migratory species. Migration is defined as "movement from one country, place, or locality to another." We have been on the move ever since the earliest humans began to spread from Africa across the Middle East, South Asia, and eventually down to Australia. Tens of thousands of years ago, our ancestors hunted and gathered food and moved on to the next destination when resources ran low. They were able to pick up their wares and search for greener pastures.

This impulse to roam and not stay tethered to one location has been making a comeback in recent years. The rise of the digital nomad lifestyle demonstrates that people are increasingly listening to their instinct to uproot and find new environments where they can flourish. It's not uncommon to see photos on social media of people working from a rustic lodge in the mountains or at a cabana on a beach. When the COVID-19 pandemic broke out in 2020, there was a sharp increase in remote workers. This allowed many people the flexibility to work in more beautiful locations and take advantage of their newfound freedom. With this freedom to roam, they could explore, go within, and figure themselves out. When things opened up more post-pandemic, these new nomads moved to other states and countries.

The popularity of the modern nomadic lifestyle is no surprise. We are simply going back to our roots. Now that we have the means to do so, we can embark on the adventures we crave deep within. Even if we don't want to hop from one destination to another, we can travel in our mind, covering more territory in the depths of our being. We can focus on learning, meditating, contemplating, creating, and contributing. Reading a good book, taking an art class, or volunteering at a soup kitchen are manifestations of our nomadic ways.

These awakened beings are heeding the call of their Nomadic Souls to transform and venture beyond the mundane to live fuller and richer lives. And by following in their footsteps, so can we.

The Nomadic Soul Archetypes

The Nomadic Soul can be better understood by getting acquainted with its two archetypes: the Curious and Pioneering Spirit and the Wise and Creative Sage.

These archetypes of the Nomadic Soul are two sides of the same coin, and both need to be expressed for us to feel whole. To be whole is to be complete, with all interrelated parts working together in harmony. These two archetypes operate in a holistic and integrated manner to help us feel connected with ourselves, other beings, and a Higher Power. When we embody them, we can align our mind, body, and heart with our purpose.

Let's examine the two archetypes of the Nomadic Soul in detail.

The Nomadic Soul Archetypes and Their Needs

THE NOMADIC SOUL

The Curious and Pioneering Spirit

The Wise and Creative Sage

The Need for Freedom

Need #1
Develop an Authentic Identity

Need #2
Explore and Learn

Need #3
Express Oneself

The Need for Connection

Need #4
Connection with Our Inner World

Need #5
Connection with Other Living Beings

Need #6
Connection with a Force Greater than Ourselves

The Curious and Pioneering Spirit Archetype

The instinct to venture beyond the confines of the old and familiar fueled our species' efforts to blaze a trail. Through inquiry, exploration, and innovation, humans continued to push boundaries and move onto higher ground with each new generation.

Whether it's building the first spacecraft to successfully land on Mars, inventing communication mediums that forever change the way we interact with each other, or concocting vaccines that inoculate us against some of the deadliest viruses, human imagination and ingenuity have shown that they know no bounds.

Except for a few eras in human history where we stood still and even regressed—such as the inquisitions, World Wars I and II, and the Dark Ages—human civilization has been on a steady growth trajectory because of an insatiable hunger for progress and enlightenment. As early as the fifth century BCE, Plato identified ideas as "the source of all things."

This rapid expansion of human civilization is due to an exceptional quality that sets us apart from other creatures: *curiosity*. We all share the craving to know and understand. It drives our growth as individuals and even our survival as species.

But where does this instinct that compels us to make big strides come from? There are two main theories behind its origin and purpose.

First, curiosity is an instinctive behavior essential for our development. Human infants have the gargantuan task of absorbing enormous amounts of information in a short period of time. For their brains to grow and develop, they must be motivated to explore and question everything in their sight. The child must learn that touching a hot iron rod can cause burns or that wandering too far away from mom and dad can lead to danger.

Curiosity also has a genetic component. While there isn't a single "curiosity gene" that causes us to explore and wonder about the world, scientists found mutations of a gene in humans called DRD4-7R, originally linked to birds and horses, and have associated it with a person's inclination to seek novelty. DRD4-7R is otherwise known as the "adventure gene," and research shows that it elicits a need to connect with a deep sense of self and to live life to the fullest.

But just because we have the desire for novelty encoded in our DNA does not mean we're all equally curious. Our level of inquisitiveness depends on how our genes interact with our environment. If curiosity is encouraged by those who raise us during our younger years, it becomes a dominant part of our personality and shapes our perspective.

Curiosity also has an intangible, sublime quality that leads us to magical frontiers. In her book *Big Magic: Creative Living Beyond Fear,* writer Elizabeth Gilbert implores us to simply follow our curiosity. "Let inspiration lead you wherever it wants," she wrote. "For most of history, people just made things, and they didn't make such a big freaking deal out of it."

It's a good thing that our ancestors didn't make a big deal about being guided by their inquisitiveness and inquiry. Without their unbridled curiosity, we wouldn't be enjoying the fruits of their labor. Charles Darwin, one of the most celebrated scientists in history, made his discoveries because he was driven by his intense love and curiosity for his subject. Even though he didn't perceive himself as intellectually gifted, his genius was sparked by an overriding desire to collect specimens and examine them.

When given the opportunity to sail around the world as a biologist on the *HMS Beagle*, Darwin was quick to take it, despite his father's disapproval. This was his chance to dive into his interests and answer burning questions about the origins of species. Intuitively he knew that if he could collect numerous specimens, he'd receive clues that could lead to the formation of his theory. He didn't care about the inconvenience and discomfort that living away from his home in England for five years would bring. He simply had to devote himself to his curiosities and find out where they might lead him.

Whether historical luminaries like Darwin were aware of it or not, they were being directed by the whispers of the Curious and Pioneering Spirit Archetype of their Nomadic Soul. Propelled by this inner force, they stumbled upon exciting vistas and made brilliant discoveries. They sensed that when they lived life through the vessel of the Nomadic Soul, there were simply no limits to how far they could see and how far they could go.

Here are some fictional characters that exemplify this archetype: Indiana Jones, Lara Croft, Captain James T. Kirk from the *Star Trek* film series, Ariel from Disney's *The Little Mermaid*, Captain Jack Sparrow from *Pirates of the Caribbean*.

Here are some historical characters that exemplify this archetype: Amelia Earhart, Christopher Columbus, Marco Polo, Diana Nyad, Anna Harriette Leonowens, Tenzing Norgay.

The Wise and Creative Sage Archetype

To understand the second archetype of the Nomadic Soul, let's travel back to ancient Rome and ancient Greece, the birthplace of democracy and the source of the greatest philosophy, science, architecture, and literature in Western civilization. Sages and scholars from both civilizations believed in a guiding spirit that was the source of creativity and genius. This spirit was also considered an intermediary between us and God—a mediator between our world and the spiritual one. The ancient Greeks referred to this entity as a "daemon," also known as *jinn* or *genii*. These wise, divine messengers from which inspiration flows point a person to their highest calling if they're willing to listen.

Throughout his writing, Socrates often mentioned his daemon and how it played a vital role in his life. In *The Apology of Socrates*, reported by Plato, Socrates said, "I am subject to a divine or supernatural experience . . . It began in my early childhood—a sort of voice which comes to me, and when it comes, it always dissuades me from what I am proposing to do."

Over time, Socrates learned to listen to this divine inner voice and act in service of it. Nothing that he did or said was without the counsel of his daemon. According to Greek-Roman writer Plutarch, Socrates showed this through his decisions to turn his back on material possessions, stay celibate, and search for wisdom. Plutarch stated that people who ignore their daemons and get distracted by passion and a drive to heed their lower desires inevitably lose this vital force. But if they listen to the voice of their divine messenger, they will be rewarded with inspiration and a life well lived.

The Romans had a slightly different take on daemons. They saw them as an energy-based force to be cultivated and honed. For them, a daemon was a personal life force that led to strokes of genius. They held special ceremonies to revitalize their spirit with new life and energy.

We can find references to this vital force in philosophical scriptures around the world. Ancient Chinese philosophers referred to it as "chi" (or qi), and Indian sages called it "prana." Even in the world of science fiction, we can find references to this guiding force. In the *Star Wars* movie franchise, this vital energy was called "the Force," a mysterious, spiritual energy field created by the cosmos that binds the galaxies together. Channeling the power of the Force fortifies the Jedi with extraordinary abilities such as tricking minds and levitating objects, among other psychic abilities.

Whether we call it a flash of insight, "the Force," or, as Albert Einstein described it, "a sudden illumination, almost a rapture," the voice of our daemon is where some of the greatest thinkers and creatives of our time took their inspiration from. The Wise and Creative Sage Archetype of the Nomadic Soul is the house of our daemon. It represents the wisest and most erudite parts of us. And, best of all, it's a resource that is always accessible to us if we tune in.

> **Here are some fictional characters that exemplify this archetype:** Yoda from *Star Wars*, Splinter from *Teenage Mutant Ninja Turtles*, Grandmother Willow in Disney's *Pocahontas*, and Hermione Granger from *Harry Potter*.

> **Here are some historical characters that exemplify this archetype:** Hypatia, the 14th Dalai Lama, Maharishi Mahesh Yogi, Pythia (the Oracle of Delphi), Toni Morrison, Lao Tzu.

When both archetypes of Nomadic Soul are fully embodied, you become a powerhouse of love, creativity, genius, compassion, sagacity—and, most importantly, you become a force for good. The lives of the six individuals featured in the subsequent Nomadic Soul case studies demonstrate the process of the unification of the Nomadic Soul archetypes and the outcome. Each one did it in their own unique way, and so can we. Their examples prove that we all have the wherewithal to reach our full potential when the essence of the Nomadic Soul archetypes emanates from our being.

The Two Fundamental Needs of the Nomadic Soul Archetypes

The Curious and Pioneering Spirit and the Wise and Creative Sage archetypes both have needs that must be fulfilled for the Nomadic Soul to have a voice.

Over time, there has been a significant shift in how we interpret and fulfill the needs of our Nomadic Souls. Deep down, we are still just as curious and creative as our predecessors were, but we've become increasingly disconnected from these yearnings, and, in the process, we have forgotten how to nurture the tremendous power that lies within us. Due to the rise of materialism and the dismissal of our mystical nature, we have lost our innate connection with the magic that lies within our bones and blood.

The ancients were aware of the needs of the Nomadic Soul and their importance because they lived in environments and cultures that were more conducive to the soul's vitality. They were tied to the land, and they knew that they had benevolent support within and around them. All they needed to do was invoke it and stay centered and grounded in their quests. They accomplished this by mastering the delicate act of balancing the two fundamental needs of the Nomadic Soul:

The Need for Freedom
The Need for Connection

The Need for Freedom flows from the Curious and Pioneering Spirit Archetype, which needs to explore, learn, and innovate. Freedom opens the gateway to move past limited thinking and see the possibilities for ourselves and what we can accomplish and contribute in our lifetime.

The Need for Connection flows from the Wise and Creative Sage Archetype, which seeks a richer, deeper, and more meaningful existence. Connection helps us transcend the superficial and calls on the most ancient and holy part of us, seeking wisdom, love, and the mystical.

The needs for Freedom and Connection are the yin and yang of our Nomadic Soul. A lack or an excess of either of these needs can cause stress and disharmony in our life.

The Six Core Needs of the Nomadic Soul

The Need for Freedom and the Need for Connection can be further broken down into subcategories of six core needs that support our well-being and the expression of our Nomadic Soul. Each of the following chapters delves more deeply into each of the six core needs, drawing on case studies from the real world and historical figures to exemplify these needs and how we can meet them in our life.

The three types of needs for Freedom are:

Freedom to develop an authentic identity
Freedom to explore and learn
Freedom to express oneself

The three types of needs for Connection are:

Connection with our inner world
Connection with other living beings
Connection with a force that's greater than ourselves

Throughout history, humanity has made giant leaps in art, science, technology, and social reform. But we have yet to embrace the process of satisfying the needs of our Nomadic Soul.

The awareness and sensitivity of our needs have gradually faded with time, and we now find ourselves in a precarious position where we must contend with life's uncertainties and the constant flux of change, with little or no counsel from our Nomadic Soul.

Before we delve into the steps we must take to revitalize the Nomadic Soul, we need to get some perspective on how we got to where we are. What caused us to drift away from our natural ways of being, leading us to our current culture of disconnection and dissatisfaction?

Restless and Uninspired: Has Society Lost Its Way?

The age of science and technology has undoubtedly made human life more comfortable, convenient, and safe—but it comes at a heavy price. Most of the pain and struggle we face today is internal, not external. After the world wars in the early twentieth century, we began living through some of the most convenient and abundant times in history. We live in safe and sanitary conditions, have access to medical facilities, face fewer conflicts, and have far more opportunities to better ourselves.

Instead of external pressures, we must deal with inner conflict and tensions. Stress, unmet expectations, low self-esteem, victim mentality, short attention spans, prejudices, and polarized ideologies are all products of our minds. We also have to deal with the same emotions that make us human: sadness, loss, and grief. Without the right perspective and practices, falling into despair is easy. This worsens as our focus has been oriented toward the outside world versus our inner world.

While racing on the road of progress, we have inadvertently tuned out the voice of the Nomadic Soul and turned up the voice of the ego. Society encourages us to focus on our careers and ambitions without encouraging us to cultivate a bountiful inner life. We've learned how to promote and advertise ourselves, but we neglect developing virtues such as sympathy, humility, and honest self-confrontation. There's a lack of depth in ego-driven people solely focused on pursuing self-interest and getting ahead of everyone. A shallow existence centered on racing to the top of the social hierarchy makes it easy to lose sight of things that matter most: love, connection, empathy, contribution, and the pursuit of knowledge and wisdom.

The exponential increase in choices confuses us and clutters our psyche. Some sources estimate that we make around thirty-five-thousand decisions daily (226.7 decisions are on food alone). Some of these decisions are calculated, some are compulsive, and some we're not conscious of making. Think about the last time you were in a grocery store. Imagine walking down the cereal aisle and observing rows and rows of different brands and types of cereal: sugar free, high fiber, low carb, organic, GMO free, and so on. The colors, designs, and nutrition labels are too much. After your eyes race up and down the aisle, all boxes appear the same, and none stand out. Unless you know what you want, you'll grab something that looks familiar or has the flashiest package.

As we become overwhelmed with all these choices, our ability to determine what supports us and what doesn't diminishes. We now have nearly unlimited choices in other settings as well, such as online dating and at work. Many of these are low-vibration choices—choices that offer instant gratification and make us entitled and self-centered. Journalist David Brooks noted this transition from a more soul-centered existence into a grandiose, ego-centered one based on data he collected for his book, *The Road to Character*. He wrote, "We have seen a broad shift from a culture of humility to the culture of what you might call the Big Me, from a culture that encouraged people to think humbly of themselves to a culture that encouraged people to see themselves as the center of the universe."

Today, we believe uploading selfies on Instagram is more fun than reading a book. Sugary treats like donuts and greasy foods like pizzas are considered more delectable than a nutritious salad. Playing the victim gets more attention online than taking responsibility for our actions. Beauty and attractiveness are increasingly based more on a person's physical appearance than their character. Situationships and hook-up culture keep us from discovering what we truly want in relationships or from healing. Fear of intimacy prevents us from immersing ourselves in a loving, committed bond.

The affluent spend millions of dollars on designer clothing and mansions rather than helping those less fortunate than them. People resort to alcohol, smoking, consuming drugs, or engaging in other addictive behaviors to escape their reality, instead of going within and addressing the issue that's causing pain and dissatisfaction.

We fear, suspect, and discriminate against people we perceive as different from us, instead of trying to understand, communicate, and collaborate with them. In his book *From Strength to Strength*, Arthur C. Brooks notes that we tend to objectify both ourselves and others, which leads us to dehumanize people. He defines "objectification" as reducing people down to one or two desirable characteristics such as money, power, or physical beauty. We then become defined by symbols of ourselves, which lowers our self-worth and life satisfaction.

It's not that our society has deliberately drifted toward feeling less whole. We simply weren't prepared for the onslaught of change and stimulation, and the explosion of options. We couldn't imagine phenomena such as the following:

- The rapid rate of change and advancement caused by new technologies—modern transportation, the internet, smartphones, and social media—all rolled out over the past century.
- The tsunami of distraction as a result of devices like smartphones and the apps in them.
- The volatile economic and political trends—like high inflation and the polarization of politics—that directly impact our everyday lives.
- The decline of communal living and robust support systems.
- The increase in consumption of processed foods and abandonment of fresh, whole foods in our diets.

As a result of these macro forces, we now increasingly:

- Experience high stress and anxiety.
- Feel distressed about the future.
- Feel lonelier than at any other time in human history.
- Worry about our security and well-being, as well as that of our loved ones.
- Don't feel like we have enough time to rest and do things that truly fulfill us.

All of this has led to the perfect storm of conditions that disconnect us from deeper aspects of our being. Despite the fact that we are the most technologically savvy and connected set of generations that's ever existed, we have never been so detached from our own emotions and intuition.

With no clear way to navigate these turbulent and high-pressure circumstances, there's been a surge in the number of people having mental, emotional, and physical breakdowns, which are just outward manifestations of our modern crisis of the soul.

Medical intuitive Caroline Myss says that "the soul always knows what to do to heal itself. The challenge is to silence the mind." Our minds now dominate our perception, and our soul has taken a backseat. Without the soul, we can't truly heal and shine our light into the world.

The younger generations, notably Gen Z and Millennials, are more susceptible to being cut off from their inner selves because they grew up in a time when grounding forces—such as meaningful traditions and supportive networks of friends and family—began to fall apart. Rituals and community were replaced by a proliferation of dry data, which presents superfluous choices emblematic of the age of consumerism and social media. Every day we are bombarded with images and videos of airbrushed celebrities and influencers uttering profanities or preaching about topics with no substance or use besides self-promotion.

According to a study published in the *Journal of Abnormal Psychology*, based on data collected from sixty thousand people by the National Survey on Drug Use and Health, the mental health of teens and young adults in the US has declined significantly since the late 2000s. The rates of depression among children between the ages of fourteen to seventeen increased by more than 60 percent between 2009 and 2017. The same study showed that more than one in eight Americans between the ages of twelve to twenty-five go through a significant depressive phase. Suicidal ideation and attempt rates also increased dramatically between 2008 and 2017. These statistics reveal the reality that adolescents are not being supported in ways that would facilitate their overall well-being and development.

Jean Twenge, author of *iGen*, a book about the effects of technology on young people's lives, wrote, "There is an overwhelming amount of data from many different sources, and it all points in the same direction: more mental health issues among American young people." While it is tough to pinpoint a single cause of the declining mental health among youth, Twenge points to one change that impacted the lives of young people more than older people: the proliferation of smartphones, which gave us access to social media, texting, and gaming. "The way young people interact and spend their free time has fundamentally changed. They spend less time with their friends in person and less time sleeping, and more time on digital media," she explained.

As bleak as these findings are, this is a glimmer of hope.

The internet has given us a global platform where we can experiment, communicate, and do so much more with our lives. It leveled the playing field and increased opportunities to find different sources of income, to network with people globally, and to share our creative gifts and contribute in bigger ways. We can carve out our own unique path to prosperity and freedom, crafting an identity online that aligns with what is true for us. Undoubtedly, there has never been a better time in human history to live on our own terms. We have much more power to control our fate than those who came before us. In the past, racism, slavery, oppression, wars, inequalities, religious dogma, lack of adequate sanitation and medical treatment, and limited access to education made it next to impossible for our progenitors to rise above the circumstances they were born into.

But our modern privileges require our discernment. As the French philosopher Voltaire put it, "With great power comes great responsibility."

Those of us who live in countries with governments that respect our personal freedoms can blaze our own trail—but it's up to us to make the best use of this opportunity. That means navigating past the distractions, noise, and social pressures that drown out the call of our Nomadic Soul, whose counsel can ensure we use this power and privilege responsibly.

Without a meaningful connection to our Nomadic Soul, we'll get lost in the void of an insipid and meaningless existence. We'll feel like boats without an anchor, floating in an ocean of untapped potential, helpless and incapable of becoming successful in our own right. No matter how majestic the surrounding seascapes appear to be or how alluring the untouched shores look, we feel stuck, unable to venture forth without the Nomadic Soul's grounded and wise presence.

"There's No Place Like Home": The Classic Journey of the Nomadic Soul

The archetypal journey of the Nomadic Soul can be found in many literary works. One of the most memorable journeys is found in one of our culture's most famous and beloved stories, *The Wonderful Wizard of Oz*. Whether you're familiar with the children's novel by L. Frank Baum or the silver screen movie starring Judy Garland based on the book, you may remember the epiphany that the main protagonist, Dorothy Gale, has upon returning to Kansas after completing her journey to the land of Oz: "There's no place like home!" The story is filled with metaphors and symbols demonstrating the archetypal journey of finding our path to our inner riches.

Not only do the beautiful sets and endearing characters transport audiences into an enchanting world of fantasy and magic, but the storyline, imagery, and characters are embedded with rich metaphors and life lessons that cohere into an overarching message of hope and inspiration.

While there are many ways to interpret Dorothy's quest to find her way back home, one way to see it is through the lens of the Nomadic Soul. Her adventure represents the quintessential journey that our Nomadic Soul urges us to take to reach a state of freedom and connectedness.

At the story's beginning, Dorothy is suddenly swept away by a tornado from her home in Kansas to the magical land of Oz. The tornado is a metaphor for the dissatisfaction and restlessness she is experiencing in her life in Kansas. She longs to be free and seek what's "over the rainbow," desires which we could interpret as her curiosity and need for personal growth. However, like many of us, she lacks the foresight to see that being uprooted from her home in Kansas was the fates' way of getting her aligned with what her soul needed.

She panics upon reaching Oz, and her only wish at that point is to find her way back home. The munchkins tell her that the only way back is to follow the yellow brick road, to go into the unknown and seek the counsel of the Wizard of Oz. The only things she has to guide her on her journey to the Emerald City, down the yellow brick road, are her ruby red slippers—her inner counsel and intuition—and a comforting companion, her dog Toto—her courage and strength.

Along the way, she meets the Tin Man, Scarecrow, and the Lion, who become her friends and allies when they decide to accompany her in her quest to find Oz. She knows that she needs the help of her new friends to reach her destination, as success is seldom a one-person journey.

Yet, upon meeting the Wizard, whom she hoped would have solutions to her problem and assuage her anxieties, she realizes that he is useless. His apparent omnipotence was nothing but a facade. Like Dorothy, many of us mistakenly believe that quick fixes and the fantasy of becoming an overnight success touted by society can magically transform our lives. The glitz and glamor of success, beauty, and fame lure us into the trap of perpetual dissatisfaction and prevent us from connecting to our own potential.

After meeting the Wizard, it becomes clear to Dorothy that it is ultimately her responsibility to deal with her predicament. Only she has the power to find her way back home. This truth is reinforced when she meets Glinda the Good Witch, a Higher Power who wisely reveals that she could have gone home at any time if only she believed in herself. The red ruby slippers are only a colorful plot device to give her the initial encouragement she needs to set off on the physical journey. Along the way, she internalizes the wisdom and lessons that she needs to use her strengths and confront her fears, which are mirrored by the Wicked Witch of the West and her henchmen.

The journey to Oz was necessary for Dorothy to learn what she needed to know to realize that home isn't a physical location or an object to be acquired but a state of being that she had to cultivate.

The key takeaway from Dorothy's story is that the home we seek is found within the deepest recesses of our Nomadic Soul. It is a state of being that we must embody by fulfilling our soul's needs and living fully expressed lives. Dorothy is able to find hers by embarking on a journey that takes her outside of her comfort zone. She proves herself by defending her friends and showing that she does not need the help of the Wizard because she has everything that she needs already within her.

Like Dorothy we can find refuge and solace whenever we encounter self-doubt, pain, loneliness, insecurities, and worries in this sacred vessel, our Nomadic Soul. It will protect us whenever we take those leaps of faith that will move us closer to our destiny.

When we give ourselves permission to explore, connect, and reflect throughout our lives, we'll discover that there really is no place like home, in the sanctuary of our Nomadic Soul. It is our path to liberation and redemption. It is where all the magic and wonder of the human experience can be found.

Personality Assessment: How Fully Expressed Is Your Nomadic Soul?

Our Nomadic Soul represents the purest, most elevated form of our consciousness. But most of us lose touch with it because of outside influences. After enduring many years of unhealthy mental conditioning, we develop limiting beliefs that undermine our nomadic essence.

Below, you are invited to take a personality assessment that will give you an inventory of your Nomadic Soul. The results from this assessment will indicate how in touch you are with your Nomadic Soul and its expressions, and which specific areas you need to work on to find your way back to your inner home.

Instructions:

1. Read each statement carefully.
2. Take as much time as you need to reflect on each statement and determine to what extent you agree with it.
3. Try to be as honest as possible in your responses, as it will affect the accuracy of your results.

Part 1: The Need for Freedom

Freedom to develop an authentic identity	Strongly Agree	Agree	Neutral	Disagree	Strongly Disagree
I feel that I am living a life based on my terms.	☐	☐	☐	☐	☐
I strive to live in alignment with my values, ethics, and personal truths.	☐	☐	☐	☐	☐
I don't allow labels and stereotypes to influence my self-image.	☐	☐	☐	☐	☐
Other people's expectations do not prevent me from doing what I feel is right for me.	☐	☐	☐	☐	☐

Freedom to explore and learn					
I like to read books, take classes, and travel to increase my knowledge and expand my horizons.	☐	☐	☐	☐	☐
I often consult mentors, experts, coaches, and consultants in times of need.	☐	☐	☐	☐	☐
I make time to explore my passions and interests.	☐	☐	☐	☐	☐
My mind is constantly buzzing with ideas and creative thoughts, which I note down.	☐	☐	☐	☐	☐

Freedom to express oneself					
Expressing my thoughts and opinions is important to me.	☐	☐	☐	☐	☐
I believe that everyone deserves the right to speak their mind.	☐	☐	☐	☐	☐
I don't hesitate to speak up for myself.	☐	☐	☐	☐	☐
I'm passionate about advocating for issues and causes that are important to me.	☐	☐	☐	☐	☐

Part 2: The Need for Connection

Connection with our inner world	Strongly Agree	Agree	Neutral	Disagree	Strongly Disagree
I am in tune with my thoughts and emotions.	☐	☐	☐	☐	☐
I trust my intuition and gut instincts.	☐	☐	☐	☐	☐
I prioritize time during my day to be still and attend to my needs.	☐	☐	☐	☐	☐
I strive to be mindful and relish the present moment.	☐	☐	☐	☐	☐

Connection with other living beings					
I have close friends, family members, and/or pets who I can count on and be myself with.	☐	☐	☐	☐	☐
I'm a member of a supportive community or multiple supportive communities.	☐	☐	☐	☐	☐
I feel empathetic about the conditions of those who are less fortunate than me and who need help.	☐	☐	☐	☐	☐
The people I'm close to support my goals and mission.	☐	☐	☐	☐	☐

Connection with a force that's greater than ourselves					
I have a spiritual practice that I engage in regularly.	☐	☐	☐	☐	☐
I feel connected to a Higher Power or something bigger than myself.	☐	☐	☐	☐	☐
I believe that I'm supported by benevolent forces that guide me on my path.	☐	☐	☐	☐	☐
Nature and other beautiful spectacles bring up a sense of awe and gratitude within me.	☐	☐	☐	☐	☐

Grading Scale

Strongly agree: 25 points
Agree: 20 points
Neutral: 15 points
Disagree: 10 points
Strongly disagree: 5 points

After calculating your points, check the appropriate category for your total score.

Interpretations of Results

Nomadic Soul Captain (440–600 points): You feel centered, strong, and empowered in your life. You are well connected to your Nomadic Soul because you prioritize your core needs. Keep up the great work and continue growing your knowledge and extending your wisdom to others.

Nomadic Soul Sailor (439–280 points): You're feeling pretty good about your life and have positive expectations about the future. You are somewhat connected to your Nomadic Soul, but there are some areas that you could improve on to move you closer to your true potential.

Nomadic Soul Drifter (279–120 points): You might feel lost and out of balance because you are disconnected from the core of your Nomadic Soul. The good news is that you're now aware of this, and you have the tools and role models to get back to your center.

What Your Results Mean

No matter which stage of evolution you are at in your Nomadic Soul journey, there is always room for improvement. If you're in a good place, reading this book will deepen your self-awareness and experiences. With each chapter, you'll be inspired and empowered to utilize your gifts to blaze your unique path in the world.

If you have been neglecting your Nomadic Soul's needs and you feel confused and lost, know that all that is about to change. Each chapter addresses the pain points specific to each need and provides steps that you can take to heal and alter the course of your life.

How This Book Can Help You

This book is for anyone longing for a more profound, more deep, and more meaningful experience of life. If you are on a path to greater psychological wholeness and you feel like something is always missing, this book will be your guide to fulfillment. While integrating the ways of the Nomadic Soul isn't for the faint of heart, it's infinitely rewarding if you do it right. You'll also be joining a small league of courageous individuals who aren't afraid to challenge the status quo and create positive change in their communities and the world.

By simply changing our thoughts and how we live, we can also positively impact the whole world. Dr. Masaru Emoto, a Japanese scientist and author who explored the effects of human consciousness on the molecular structure of water, demonstrated the influence of thoughts, prayers, and intentions on water. In his book *The Hidden Messages in Water*, Emoto writes, "Water has a memory and carries within it our thoughts and prayers. As you yourself are water, no matter where you are, your prayers will be carried to the rest of the world."

We are all works in progress with areas we can improve on. For example, you might be tuned in to your inner world because of the time and attention you invest in your personal development. But all the time that you spend on yourself may have caused you to lose focus on your relationships. Not spending time with friends and family can lead to feelings of isolation and loneliness. In this case, you would need to focus on your Nomadic Soul's need for connection with other beings. You'll be guided on the types of relationships available and how to find and build meaningful connections that enhance your life.

Refer to your assessment results to determine which areas you need to work on. Pay attention to the sections where you scored the lowest and refer to the chapters highlighting those issues. However, to get the most from your growth experience, read the book in its entirety first. Getting a big-picture perspective on the characteristics of a Nomadic Soul and its needs can make your transformation deeper and long lasting.

Each chapter works in conjunction with the others to offer you perspectives, frameworks, and tools to overcome blocks and move forward with purpose. *The Nomadic Soul* is a practical guide to your personal achievement and fulfillment that will help reshape your vision of the world and your place within it.

Be patient with yourself as you implement changes and learn new thought patterns. It takes time and commitment to plant these new seeds within us and see them sprout. If you create the right habits, routines, and accountability systems to help yourself stay on track, you'll eventually get there. Remember, the rewards of life are in the journey of our becoming, not the destination itself.

Each of the following chapters opens with case studies of six well-known figures from modern history who lived with fully expressed Nomadic Souls. Together, we will distill the wisdom and lessons from their life stories and then explore theories, exercises, and practices to better meet each Nomadic Soul need in the "Digging Deep" sections. The guidance you'll gain is tangible and pragmatic and can be easily applied in everyday life.

In the first part of the book, we'll go in depth into the three facets of the Nomadic Soul's need for freedom, while in the second half of the book, we will dive deep into the three facets of our need for connection. Each of the chapters works together to bring you closer to your true essence. Each will provide you with the knowledge and tools you'll need to enhance your mindset and create a lifestyle and value system that aligns with the six needs of your Nomadic Soul.

As you go through this transformation, your ability to empathize with others will be enhanced. Nomadic Souls are deeply aware that everything is interconnected, and we should demonstrate sensitivity and tolerance toward people of all races, cultures, and nationalities.

Like Nelson Mandela, an exemplar Nomadic Soul, said, "No one is born hating another person because of the color of his skin, or his background, or his religion. People must learn to hate, and if they can learn to hate, they can be taught to love, for love comes more naturally to the human heart than its opposite."

Given the unsettled state of global affairs and a society plagued by narcissism, shallowness, entitlement, and victim mentality, the world needs more conscious, selfless, and kind people. We need to awaken to our inherent goodness and become bridges of peace and unity, to shift humanity in a positive direction. When you embody your Nomadic Soul, you'll become part of this collective movement to change the world in your own unique way. But change must first start from within.

Let's begin this exciting voyage toward expansion and personal discovery.

PART 1

Freedom

NEED #1

Develop an Authentic Identity

We are multidimensional beings, capable of molding our character at any stage during our soul journey. Our identity is fluid and malleable, and we should continue to evolve and enhance it to realize our highest potential.

Case Study: Viktor Frankl (1905–1997)

"Everything can be taken from a man, but one thing:
the last of the human freedoms—to choose
one's attitude in any given set of circumstances,
to choose one's own way."

Viktor Frankl lost his entire family in the Nazi concentration camps during World War II. His father died of exhaustion, while his mother and brother were murdered in the gas chambers. His wife, Tilly, died of typhus after she was forced by the Nazis to abort their unborn child. Anyone else who endured such loss and pain would drown in the depths of despair, but Viktor chose to become stronger for it, using tragedy to fortify his spirit.

Viktor witnessed firsthand the depths of man's cruelty and injustice in the concentration camps. Despite the torturous and debilitating conditions he was subjected to while at the camps in Auschwitz and Dachau, Viktor continued to work on his manuscript and thesis on the meaning of life. As he observed the degradation and brutality around him, he noticed that some inmates died even though they could have endured. He theorized that their demise was due to their lack of purpose.

Through his observations, Viktor admitted that people want power and pleasure but are ultimately driven by a need for meaning in their lives. As he witnessed in the concentration camps, it is the search for meaning that keeps someone alive when everything else has been taken away. Armed with this knowledge and his experience as a psychotherapist, Viktor tried to help those imprisoned in the camps connect with their purpose even when they had lost all hope and will to live. For some, their "why" involved unfinished business or the hope they could reunite with the child waiting for them upon liberation. Others had great faith they could lean on when things got especially trying and challenging. Viktor concluded that meaning can be found in any life situation if we're willing to dig deep.

Viktor attended to the psychological crises experienced by those imprisoned in concentration camps by organizing a first-response team for the shocked new arrivals in an effort to stave off suicide. He could have focused only on his own well-being and survival in the camps, but instead he wanted to help other people no matter what he was going through personally. From early on, he realized that helping people was his purpose and central to his identity.

Viktor contracted typhoid fever while imprisoned. With determination and his medical knowledge, he survived until the American troops liberated the inmates from the oppression and torture of the Nazis in April 1945. In the aftermath of his liberation, Viktor concluded his research on the meaning of life and wrote a book titled *Man's Search for Meaning*. The book was a massive hit, selling a whopping nine million copies.

Many of us would struggle to live a normal life if we had gone through what Viktor did, but he never gave in to the identity labels placed upon him by his Nazi oppressors. No matter how much the Nazis vilified and tortured him and his people, he did not allow oppression to shift his attitude and dampen his spirit. Their opinion and treatment of him did not define him, because he knew who he was deep down inside. In his book, Viktor recalled how the officers in the concentration camp examined each new prisoner and pointed them to go left or right. The stronger and more able-bodied men were sent to the right line to work. The 90 percent directed to the left line were sent to perish in the gas chambers. Viktor was sent to the right. In the fields, he and surviving prisoners were humiliated by their captors. They were told to remove all their clothes, they were shaved from head to toe, and they were sent to the showers. Viktor begged one of the guards to let him keep a draft of the psychology book he was working on, to no avail.

Everything that the prisoners had was taken away. With everything gone, they were forced to find levity. A grim sense of humor overtook them, and they began to make fun of themselves and each other. Viktor said that humor was their souls' way of coping with the crushing reality. They stood shivering in chilly autumn air with no clothes, titles, possession, or family. Even their names were taken from them by the Nazi officers, and they were reduced to numbers. Each prisoner had to reckon with a daunting question: *Who are we now?*

In their new naked human existence, they had to redefine themselves. They had to get in touch with the raw truth of their humanity, and the only way that they could do that was by searching for purpose—a reason to live. No matter what other people do or say to us, we have independence of mind to choose our own way and a persona that aligns with that. In *Man's Search for Meaning*, Viktor wrote, "Everything can be taken from a man but one thing: the last of the human freedoms—to choose one's attitude in any given set of circumstances, to choose one's own way."

This was not Viktor's first experience of war. Born in Vienna in 1905, Viktor was a child during World War I. In those war years, he witnessed large-scale combat that brought about severe deprivation and damage. He knew how another war would likely play out. As a well-known Jewish doctor, he had managed to obtain a visa for the United States to escape the Nazis, but he couldn't bear the thought of relocating to a different country and escaping the threats of war while his parents endured the tragedy without any help or assistance. The pain of leaving them behind was too great to bear, and it went against his ideals. To stay in integrity with himself and what he stood for, he remained in Austria, despite the risk of becoming a prisoner and facing death.

During his formative years, Viktor developed an interest in studying medicine and eventually became a physician. As a young boy, he was wise beyond his years and loved socializing with people and assisting those in distress. While in high school, he was actively involved with the Young Socialist Workers organization. By 1921, based on findings from personal research and observation, he gave his first lecture at the age of fifteen on the meaning of life. There he began to express the worldview that people needed to discover answers within themselves.

As his studies evolved, he became interested in studying science and human behavior, attending applied psychology conferences to build on his knowledge of the subject. His zest for pursuing his passion of psychology drove him to conduct comprehensive studies and write essays on human nature. His work was noticed by Sigmund Freud, with whom he developed a friendship. They corresponded by post. Soon after completing high school and before entering university, Viktor met Freud in person. It was an epic meeting between mentor and mentee, where Freud discussed some of his controversial ideas of psychoanalysis with the young scholar. Their interactions completely transformed Viktor's view on human behavior and further stimulated his interest in the subject.

He seized every opportunity to further his knowledge on these subjects. He read books, engaged in research, and sought mentors who could guide him, as well as peers who offered support and feedback that helped him become aware of blind spots in his research. Taken together, these actions motivated Viktor to reach his full potential and use what he learned to help others develop theirs. Even during times of stress and strife, he maintained a steady focus on what was most important to him: his family, his work as a researcher and psychoanalyst, and his mission to serve those in need.

His meeting with Freud inspired Viktor to write an article titled "Psychotherapy and Weltanschauung," in which he examined the frontier between psychotherapy and philosophy, focusing on the fundamental question of the meaning of life and the values of human beings. These would later form the focal point of most of his life's work.

In Vienna, where Viktor grew up, student suicide was a regular occurrence. This trend concerned him and inspired him to focus his studies on suicide and depression. Between 1928 and 1929, Viktor began organizing free counseling centers for teenagers based in Vienna and six other cities throughout Austria to improve their mental health. He believed that reaching our highest potential is the ultimate goal of every individual. For him, suicide among these young students was symptomatic of the pressures on them born out of a search for meaning and identity. Viktor knew that it was at this age that individuals struggled the most with developing their own sense of self. He was confident that the tension between the young students' search for identity and the need to conform to societal demands was responsible for their breakdowns. He made up his mind to do everything within his means to stem the tide.

He began organizing a special counseling program at the end of the school term around schools in Vienna. Such was the brilliance of Viktor's methods that the number of student suicides dropped significantly. While earning his degree in medicine, his career began to blossom, and Viktor rose to prominence in Vienna as his methods for treating suicidal ideation were proven effective. He attended to thousands of patients annually. His professional services were so much in demand that he established his own private practice.

However, in the midst of making a positive impact and restoring hope in the youth, catastrophe struck. His world came crashing down almost at the same speed it took off. Just one year after he established his private practice, war broke out again when Adolf Hitler invaded Austria. But this time, the war was bigger and more severe than the one he had witnessed in his childhood. Even amid the horrific circumstances he found himself in, he still found a way to serve the prisoners in the concentration camps. No matter how hard the Nazi captors tried to disrupt his circumstances, he didn't allow them to disturb the sanctity of his inner world. He knew who he was: a healer and hope-giver to those in despair. By serving others, he reinforced his individuality and his core values.

Despite the emotional trauma from losing his family members and enduring the unimaginable hardships of living in the camps, he persisted in his mission after World War II. He took up the role of director at the Vienna Neurological Polyclinic the following year, and he held the position for twenty-five years. He also laid the foundation for logotherapy, a form of therapy based on the premise that humans are intrinsically motivated by the need to find meaning, which Viktor argued could be found in even the worst of situations.

One successful application of logotherapy occurred when Viktor helped an elderly man process the loss of his wife. In their sessions together, he helped the grieving man see how there was purpose in her death, changing his perspective. The man was comforted by the idea that, by his wife passing first, she was spared the pain of losing her husband and dealing with his death. Through successful cases like this, Viktor proved that finding purpose strengthens resilience, even in the face of loss and challenge. When faced with adversity, it serves us well to reinvent ourselves and find a new perspective on life that can uplift us.

In 1947, Viktor married Eleonore Schwindt, and they welcomed their daughter in December of the same year. He obtained his PhD and would go on to author several books. Later in his life, he received worldwide recognition, accolades, and admiration, but he never forgot where he came from. He knew that his story played a critical role in shaping who he was and the impact he wanted to have on future generations long after he was gone.

The circumstances surrounding the life of Viktor Frankl were, undoubtedly, extraordinary. He lived through a turbulent era in human history, witnessing dreadful atrocities and injustice. Yet, no matter what was happening around him, Viktor remained true to his ideals and did not let his Nazi oppressors' demeaning labels define him. His dedication to broadening his knowledge of human behavior gave him the tools and insights he needed to protect his sense of self in the most difficult circumstances imaginable. From early on in his life, he was aware of his strengths, flaws, and interests. He was in tune with his core essence and the purpose of his journey on Earth.

Based on his experiences and his studies, he concluded that every human, regardless of race, color, or nationality, has a deep need for meaning and self-actualization. We can fulfill this yearning for purpose by engaging in a life of inquiry and introspection, maintaining self-awareness, and engaging in personal development. According to Viktor, meaning is not some abstract notion that will apply to everyone. Rather, where and how we find meaning in our lives is unique to each individual and their specific circumstances. In his book, he presents three ways we can find meaning:

- Through work, by creating or doing something.
- Through love, by experiencing something or encountering someone.
- Through suffering, by the attitude we take toward unavoidable suffering.

He points out that suffering is often the road to salvation and self-growth. Instead of avoiding it, we must see it as a source of wisdom. We build character, empathy, and strength from overcoming pain more than we do from our happy, pleasant moments.

Throughout Viktor's professional life, and even his personal life, he prioritized guiding people to find their deeper purpose. In the process, he discovered himself and crystallized his mission. Despite the challenges and obstacles of his time, he never swayed from the path that his heart was set on. As someone who was in touch with his Nomadic Soul, Viktor Frankl lit the way to self-realization for everyone with his wisdom and kindness. He proved that the transition from a limited to an expansive sense of self must always begin with knowing who we are and what we're willing to fight for.

Understanding Our Need: Who Am I?

True Identity

When most people are asked the question *Who are you?,* they usually respond by describing the professional and personal roles that they play in their life. They say things like, "I'm an accountant, doctor, carpenter, father, brother, aunt, mother, etc."

While all of these labels may be correct, they barely scratch the surface of our true identity. Such labels do not do justice to the kaleidoscope of traits, hopes, fears, and aspirations that make up our character. What they reveal to others is only the tip of the iceberg, while the deeper details—our true nature—remain hidden from view.

We attempt to project a public façade that's flawless because society categorizes us based on surface appearances. Other people like to put us into boxes so that it's easier for them to size us up based on fixed social parameters like what we do for a living, how we dress, how we talk, how we move, how we look, our net worth, and where we're from. For instance, a man in a medical apron is identified as a doctor, while a college professor might easily be determined by their glasses and contemplative countenance.

If we lack a sense of identity, we begin to see ourselves through the lens of other people and allow our individuality to be limited by labels. But these social veneers are not the real us. Our identity isn't what we do for a living. Our identity isn't what our fathers tell us that you can be. It isn't what culture expects us to be. Your identity is defined by you and how you feel about yourself. Your identity goes a lot deeper. It is your core essence minus the social conditioning. And you'll find it in the realm of Nomadic Soul.

When we arrived in this world as babies, our minds were blank slates, but after enduring many years of mental conditioning, we lost sight of our authenticity and our potential. When we were children, we believed that we could be anything that our hearts desired—astronaut, athlete, pilot, movie star, etc. But somewhere along the way we developed limiting beliefs and allowed other people and circumstances to dictate the course of our lives and tell us who we should and shouldn't be. Well-intentioned parents, teachers, and society in general help us to become responsible, grown-up adults, but they can also unwittingly squeeze out all those wonderful youthful attributes such as curiosity, wonder, and an openness to the world.

These figures can sometimes box us into a fixed way of being based on rules, expectations, and cultural norms that we need to abide by to function well in society. As we grow up, we lose touch with that pure consciousness of our Nomadic Soul that we were born with, which contained the seeds of our becoming. If we allow ourselves to be guided by it, our true identity will gracefully reveal itself to us like a butterfly emerging from a cocoon. We'll get intuitive hunches that nudge us in the right direction and attract favorable events and people and draw them into our space. Viktor Frankl was aware of his identity from an early age and stayed true to his mission, even when the Nazi oppressors in the concentration camps tried to beat it out of him and strip him of his dignity. The stronger his will, the more he felt guided in his next steps, even when conditions around him were deteriorating.

The core essence of the Nomadic Soul is the truth about a person that can be defined and embodied only by someone who is self-aware. It requires answering this fundamental question: "What is it that makes you, *you*?" When you think of famous people in history, such as Leonardo da Vinci, Martin Luther King Jr., or Mother Teresa, you instantly have a strong sense of their personality, values, and interests. Regardless of their morality or their principles, their words and actions made it crystal clear what they stood for.

They communicated their values to the masses on massive platforms, where they could advocate for their agendas and voice their thoughts. Even though most of us do not have a platform of the same scale and reach as these well-known individuals, we have our own intimate stages of self-discovery, with an audience composed of our family, friends, and coworkers, who witness what we do and say in our daily lives.

The reality is that almost all of us put on a social mask when we're out in the world and under scrutiny. More often than not, this persona seldom reflects our genuine traits. As Nomadic Souls, our objective is to avoid portraying a false self and to strive to be as authentic as possible. In doing so, we stay in integrity with our truth. People will perceive us as genuine and trustworthy. As if by magic, this opens up doors for serendipitous events and opportunities to enter our personal and professional lives.

We use the word "essence" to describe our identity because it captures the nuances of our character and its limitless nature. We are not a laundry list of qualities. Rather, we are complex entities that are constantly growing, evolving, and shifting. Throughout our lives, we will have to contend with contradictory thoughts, emotions, and priorities. And we all have a light and dark side to us.

For instance, Albert Einstein is considered one of the most outstanding scientists whose contributions changed how we understand the world and the course of science itself. But, by his own admission, he was socially inept and often disrespectful toward the women he was involved with. Similarly, we, too, have unsavory sides. We must respect the reality of our polarities and contradictions and realize that they're all part of our identity. We are an organic blend of qualities and affinities that are in a constant state of flux and evolution.

Spiritual teacher Mark Nepo says that there is a paradox to having a self that carries some form of spirit within it. In *Surviving Storms*, he wrote, "For as human beings, our being is infinite and unlimited, but our humanness is very finite and limited. And so, there is a common, inner tension, as we soar and plod at the same time. The being in us flies like a hawk. It knows nothing of the ground. It sees the terrain but glides above all its obstacles. But the human in us walks like a horse and must climb over everything. It plods along, a step at a time, and must traverse everything in its way."

According to Nepo, the way to overcome this tension is by knowing our true self and keeping our being and our humanness "kindly tethered" so that they can work together to create harmony within us. This tethering occurs when we dig deeper into our Nomadic Soul.

How We Develop Identity

Each of us has a unique identity. It's shaped in many ways by different forces. There are a number of visible and invisible factors that play a role in forming identity. That's why the process isn't linear, and its expression is unpredictable. Like a canyon carved into a rock formation by a river, we won't know how long it will take or how the shape of our identity will change over time.

Most experts in psychology claim that our childhood environment and experiences have a monumental impact on our identity formation. At this stage of development, our minds are open and malleable, and we absorb everything around us like sponges. As we grow up, we become more resistant to outside influences, and the behavioral patterns formed during our younger years become entrenched. That's why we often say, "You can't teach an old dog new tricks."

Several prominent psychologists have developed theories that outline the stages of identity formation, which involve several cognitive, social, and moral influences.

- Sigmund Freud suggested that personality is developed in stages related to specific erogenous zones through his theory of psychosexual development.
- According to Erik Erikson, identity is "psycho-social"; there is an ongoing conflict between what a person needs and what society needs from the person.

- Jean Piaget's theory on cognitive development states that children play an active role in developing their personality during their formative years.
- Lawrence Kohlberg focused on the growth of moral thought in children. He built on the two stages proposed by Piaget and expanded the theory to include six stages. He claimed that a person's moral development evolves throughout their lifespan.

Contemporary psychologists have pointed out that while these theories are valid, highlighting the pivotal role that our upbringing and environment have in identity development, they are missing a vital piece of the puzzle: the effects of our DNA, the genetic traits we've inherited.

Research now suggests that our genetic propensities play a far more prominent role in our personality development than our upbringing does. In a well-known study known as the "Minnesota Study of Twins Reared Apart," researchers observed 350 pairs of twins between 1979 and 1999. The participants included both fraternal and identical twins who were either raised in one household or separate households. The results revealed that the twins turned out to be very similar in their dispositions whether they were raised together or not, proving the significant role that genes play in personality development.

While our genetics carry the blueprint for our body functions, our basic temperament, and our personality traits, DNA does not determine our destiny. We do. Even though we are made up of countless biochemical compounds and trillions of condensed cells that form our tissues and organs, our identity is an aspect developed from our own effort and conscious will.

As humans, we are self-aware, conscious, and capable of creating stories, value systems, fictitious entities, and abstract concepts, such as the authority of nations and the value of monetary currency, to give order to our world. This meaning-making process includes the perspectives we develop about ourselves. In his book *Sapiens*, author Yuval Noah Harari wrote, "Sapiens rule the world because only they can weave an intersubjective web of meaning: a web of laws, forces, entities and places that exist purely in their common imagination. This web allows humans alone to organize crusades, socialist revolutions and human rights movements."

The bottom line is that our identity is based on a set of belief systems centered on who we *believe* we are instead of *who we are* and *how we are*. Our identity is a mental construct that stems from our thoughts and attitudes. No matter what type of genetic cards you were dealt or what kind of environment you grew up in, the choice is ultimately yours when it comes to selecting which influences and experiences you choose to integrate into your identity.

Identity Influencers

Our identity is like a colorful mosaic, composed of intricate parts that form the entirety of our being. If we want to remove, modify, or add on to our identity, we should be aware of the foundation of our character.

From the time we are children, we have absorbed everything that's surrounded us. We become products of our experiences. We need to be in touch with underlying influences on our identity to know how they impact our choices and self-perception. Without a defined sense of self, we have no firm grounding in our ideology and are more likely to take on others' views and beliefs. These beliefs can become attached to our core identity. Often, we cling to our beliefs, even if they are harmful and destructive.

For example, those who identify with the ideologies of Nazism adopt an attitude of ignorance, fear, and hatred. They may reveal these beliefs in the form of hate crimes. In contrast, a person identifying as an animal rights activist may choose to be a vegetarian and volunteer at animal shelters, thereby positively influencing society. Even though these ideologies are on opposite ends of the moral spectrum, the process of adopting a genocidal ideology like Nazism is the same as the one that drives someone to become an animal rights activist.

Both types of people developed a passion for their chosen ideologies, making that ideology a part of their identity and value system. To avoid stepping into fear-based ideologies that don't serve us or the world around us, we must take an inventory of the people, origins, events, and environments that shaped us and evaluate them based on an ethical and moral framework.

Your identity influencers can be categorized into four areas:

- **Official/Inherited**—Identity influencers you inherited by birth and the circumstances you were born into. Examples include the following: generational traits, national identity, physical appearance, birth order traits, health conditions, and family legacy.
- **Professional**—Identity influencers that you've earned through your profession and vocation. Examples include the following: professional titles, college alum affiliations, and professional associations.

- **Social or Collective Identity**—Identity influencers you've gained through your association with groups you belong to. Examples include the following: political parties, religious and spiritual communities, and sports teams.
- **Aspirations or Hobbies**—Identity influencers connect to things you're passionate about that you like to do in your spare time. These are activities that energize you and give meaning to your life. Examples include the following: hobbies, creative side hustles, sporting activities, volunteer work, and online content that you like to consume.

As you read this list, see if any of them stand out to you. Some of these attributes might overlap. For example, your morals could be informed by your religious beliefs. In a later section, you'll have a chance to evaluate the impact that each one has on your identity.

Your identity is multidimensional, and each part is shaped by different sources. Your dream to become a teacher may have come from a favorite high school teacher who inspired you with her empathy and attention to detail. Your goal to master the moves of a hip-hop dancer may have taken form after watching a Beyoncé music video. Your love for fashion might have been sparked while working part time at a clothing retail store. You may have become an Old Hollywood movie buff after you got hooked on those films during a course you took in college. All of the circumstances and people that enter your life have the potential to add a stroke to the canvas of your personality.

Four Reasons Why We Need a Defined and Self-Informed Identity

People in touch with their Nomadic Soul have high self-awareness and a defined identity. They know who they are and what they stand for, but they're also able to reinvent themselves along the way. It's not always easy to stay the course, as many distractions and temptations will sway you from your path. Knowing why it is essential to be in the driver's seat of our identity development will motivate you and keep you alert as you go through the various phases of your life.

1. To stand up for ourselves

We have no control over the circumstances that we were born into, nor can we know what will happen to us over the course of our lives. But we can rewrite our story and configure our identity in response to what occurs. When we realize that we have this power and use it, we won't have to rely on the opinions of our peers, family, and society.

If we're weak in our will and our priorities aren't integrated into our being, it's easy to fall into the trap of trying to meet the expectations of people who don't respect our individuality and who refuse to give us the liberty to explore our feelings and ambitions. Motivational speaker Jim Rohn famously said, "If you don't design your own life plan, chances are you'll fall into someone else's plan. And guess what they have planned for you? Not much."

Without a clear self-identity, we can succumb to external pressure from several entities like the following:

Communities with a heavy tribal mentality

These communities will try their best to make us conform to the collective identity and prevent us from behaving in ways that are not in alignment with the group. A fear-based mentality drives these individuals to maintain order by curtailing the freedom and rights of others. This type of ideology is commonly associated with cults and extremist groups that try to brainwash followers with their dogma.

An egregious example is the Peoples Temple cult mass murder-suicide in the South American nation of Guyana on November 18, 1978. Under the direction of the founder Jim Jones, many followers willingly drank a poison-laced punch. Others were forced to drink it. More than nine hundred cultists, including over two hundred children, lost their lives that day.

Social groups with this type of fear-based mentality believe that controlling their members will keep them safe from harm and that holding onto traditions will prevent the perceived bad influence of outsiders from seeping into their circle. This is especially important for those who live in traditional societies where rules must be strictly followed. Living in a mold with little room for individuality causes people to become what they are not.

These groups may expect their members to follow a specific dress code, hairstyle, or marital behaviors that adhere to the community's values. They believe that anything that shakes the status quo of their group identity is a threat that must be eliminated. But when you take charge of molding your identity, you protect yourself from societal pressure that tries to change the identity of people so that they can fall in line with what's acceptable to them.

Family

The pressure to conform can be present in families as well. Parents who try to push their own identities—their dreams, hopes, and aspirations—on their children often create identity blocks for their kids. Even though most who raise children mean well and think that they are doing the right thing, they don't realize that they could be blocking their children from blossoming into the person that they are meant to be. For example, if a person grew up in a family where the past couple of generations of professionals were lawyers, they might be expected to continue the family legacy by taking on the profession. In this case, their family might be limiting the development of their true self-identity. Their family's expectations would not be a problem if the child had a genuine interest in law, but if it's not something they enjoyed doing, they'll be living a life of servitude and regret.

Peer pressure

Societal vices like addictions, fundamentalism, and violence are often spread due to negative social influences and peer pressure. A person who constantly works and interacts with particular types of people will often imitate what they do, even if those traits aren't reflective of who they really are. If you live in a poor, often dangerous neighborhood where gun violence and drug trading are the norm and have no access to proper education, it will not seem unnatural for you to partake in these activities, because that would be all you know. Poorly resourced neighborhoods offer fewer educational and professional opportunities to climb out of the circumstances you find yourself in. Sometimes conforming to the ways of the people in your immediate surroundings is critical to your survival, and you know that you need to take steps to protect yourself and your loved ones. If there are chances of being held at gunpoint, you need to be equipped to handle it accordingly.

2. To make the right choices

From our profession to our food preferences, every choice we make is filtered through the lens of our identity. We need to play an active role in crafting and evolving an identity so that our choices stay aligned with our Nomadic Soul and its purpose during this lifetime. Our responsibility is to manage the deeper aspects of who we are, and we should do everything that we can to facilitate this process.

From a young age, children should be encouraged to follow their curiosity and explore different roles and activities that are positive and enriching. Through trial and error, they will gradually realize what works for them and what doesn't. Like the comforting sensation of a shoe that fits well, our soul will alert us when we have found something to pursue further.

Here are some basic indicators that you've stumbled on something that aligns with your Nomadic Soul:

- It comes naturally to you.
- You saw glimpses of your interest in it when you were younger.
- It empowers you and raises your self-esteem.
- It's easy for you to learn.
- You look forward to doing it. It fulfills you.
- It improves the lives of others around you and brings them joy.

- You get into the zone when engaged in it.
- Time flies when you're immersed in it.
- You can do it all day, even if you don't get compensated for it.

We must engage in self-discovery as early as possible because we tend to resist changing how we see ourselves as we age and mature. We are less willing to create shifts in our identity, even if our personality and our choices feel out of sync with our soul's mission.

3. To maintain solid self-esteem

Besides making better-informed choices, having a coherent identity strengthens our self-esteem. It makes us confident and self-assured in the presence of others. Our assuredness protects us from tyrants and tricksters who might try to convince us to join causes and groups without considering our preferences and needs. These influences can range from a pushy salesperson trying to get us to buy their products to cult leaders brainwashing us to leave our homes and loved ones to promote their ideology.

We can stand firm in the face of bullies and naysayers who try to put us down and make us second-guess ourselves because of our beliefs. Nikola Tesla, one of the most prolific scientists of all time, faced slander and persecution during his lifetime. Still, he did not allow it to diminish his confidence in his capabilities. He said, "All that was great in the past was ridiculed, condemned, combated, suppressed—only to emerge all the more powerfully, all the more triumphantly from the struggle." Nothing can sidetrack us when we are transparent and resolute in our pursuits.

We will stand, proud and strong, like a sturdy oak tree, convinced of our worth and values.

4. To appreciate the different facets of our identity

Our identities are like loose coats that we can put on and take off. It's okay to wear different coats on different occasions. Because we are multifaceted, we will have several suitable coats for every context in our life and the different roles that we play in our professional and personal lives. For example, we'll be a Red Sox fan when hanging out with our buddies, a loving mother with our children, an enterprising manager at the office, and a sci-fi fan at the movies. Switching between these different identity coats is normal social behavior. The key is to be conscious of these various identities and ensure that each one reflects your truth and contributes to creating a coherent whole.

One way that our Nomadic Soul can instruct us as we develop our identity is through our instincts. In his book *Instinct: Unleashing Your Natural Drive for Ultimate Success*, T. D. Jakes refers to our instincts as the treasure map for our soul's satisfaction. Jakes defines instinct as "a genetically hardwired tendency, a behavior that's built in and automatic, not learned or conditioned." When refined and harnessed, our instincts can direct us toward a more joyful, productive, and satisfying life. Your mission is to listen to your instincts so that they can guide you to orchestrate the right conditions to tap into the natural strengths of your distinct and unique self.

Depending on how self-aware you are, you may have had several experiences where you encountered different aspects of your identity. Perhaps it was through a stroke of creative insight or a sense of timelessness when taking a walk in the wilderness. It might even have been a time when you were swept with feelings of unconditional love. Your true identity represents the deeper part of you that originates from your Nomadic Soul. It's the part of you that is free from social and cultural conditioning, old memories, emotional ups and downs, and the influence of others. It's found during times when you are still and aware of the aliveness in the present moment. This self-knowledge is intuitive—it's derived from a sense of knowing, rather than the tangible reality we perceive through our senses.

To discover our true selves, we don't want to get attached to our identity labels. When we cling on to our identities, we operate out of fear and ego. This can trap us in dysfunctional patterns and even make us prone to displaying extreme behaviors, as we have commonly seen in the long history of national and religious warfare. There is no need to force your beliefs onto others. What works for you may not work for others and vice versa. Respecting others' individuality is just as important as upholding our own truth.

Digging Deep: How to Be Who You Really Are

How to Meet Our Need to Develop an Authentic Identity

Now that we know what characterizes an authentic identity and what gets in the way of expressing our authentic selves, we can examine how we develop and showcase our identity to the rest of the world. In other words, we're going to put our *authenticity into action*.

But how exactly does one embrace their authenticity? The answer is by going within. Becoming a genuine person requires us to look underneath the hood and examine all parts of us—the good, bad, and ugly—from a place of love and acceptance. Not many people are willing to do this because they're afraid of what they may find lurking in the shadows. They would rather live in denial than face the unpleasantness of the parts of themselves that society told them are broken and forbidden. It's much easier to wear a false mask and pretend that everything is okay than it is to come to terms with our demons and resolve the painful memories we have not addressed yet.

But our vulnerability makes us human, and that's something we need to acknowledge if we are to reach a place of wholeness. It's a truth that every Nomadic Soul learns to accept. If you embark on this vital part of the Nomadic Soul's journey, you'll soon realize that embracing every aspect of your being is not as scary as most people imagine it to be. Even if some parts of the process are difficult, it will ultimately liberate you. It's like ripping off a Band-Aid that's concealing a wound—you can take steps to heal it. There is nothing more freeing than being your genuine self and living by what you believe in. In doing so, you will step into your power and fully own it.

Developing an Authentic Identity Using the Onion Methodology

An effective way of constructing an authentic identity is to liken the layers of our identity to layers of an onion. At the center of the onion lies our core essence, which hardly ever changes unless we go through some major traumatic life event where we endure insurmountable hardships and emotional turmoil. However, we have the capacity to hold on to our identity in the face of major disruption, as Viktor Frankl did. For the most part, our innate qualities and basic temperament remain unchanged. It's that *nature* aspect of us, if we're talking in terms of nature versus nurture.

Our core identity is surrounded by several layers that form over our lifetime as we accumulate experiences and knowledge and are exposed to other people's influence. Each of these layers represents a distinct aspect of our individuality, which we have willingly or unknowingly assimilated. Think of the outer layers of the onion as the *nurture* aspect of our personality. The conditioned part of ourselves reflects our upbringing, education, life experiences, and other influences that have played a key role in shaping us.

The Identity Onion

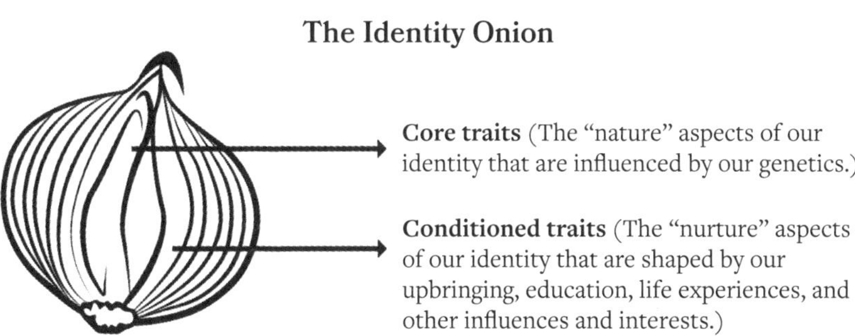

Before we get into the process of peeling off the layers to access our core essence, we need to work on developing one vital skill: our capacity for self-awareness. That is the ability to be conscious of the world inside you: your feelings, thoughts, sensations, images, memories, and experiences. Self-awareness is vital if you want to understand and evaluate your behavior accurately. With built-in awareness, we strengthen our ability to define ourselves and develop a coherent self-concept.

Ultimately, you determine your self-concept, and you can alter it if you ever feel the need to do so. The more you learn about yourself and your behavior, the more mindful you become of the patterns that do not serve you. By becoming an objective observer of your tendencies, you'll become the leader in your life who can make powerful and purposeful moves. This section will help you cultivate an innate awareness of who you are so that your outer identity is reflection of your Nomadic Soul.

Studies in quantum physics have proven that everything is simply energy stored in mass particle form. This includes humans. As energy-based beings, each of us has a unique frequency and blueprint, and it is our job to get a clear sense of what our field is so that we can emanate its light in its full magnificence.

The Identity Onion methodology is a way to create an authentic identity that involves a three-step process in which we unravel the distinct parts of our identity by engaging in the process of self-reflection, education, and rituals. It's an inside-out approach fueled by curiosity, openness, and non-judgment.

As creatures of habit who take comfort in routine and predictability, we tend to stick with predictable thought patterns, behaviors, and affinities that we've grown accustomed to.

But in order to step into our authenticity, we need to step out of the rut and grow into what feels right for us.

Our realness lies in the subtle and unseen parts of us: our feelings, thoughts, and natural predispositions. This ethereal part of identity is where our Nomadic Soul dwells. We unveil it when we dig deep and reflect on who we are and who we are becoming. From a rational perspective, defining those aspects of ourselves can be confusing. We need intuitive-based tools to work in tandem with our logical minds to build a coherent image.

Below is a step-by-step guide for knowing yourself more fully.

There are three steps to peeling back the layers to reveal your authenticity:

Step 1: Self-analysis (how you see yourself)

Step 2: Getting feedback from others (how others see you)

Step 3: Develop authenticity habits and practices (how to live a life that best represents you)

Take your time moving through each step, using the journaling prompts to facilitate self-reflection.

Step 1: Self-analysis

In this section, you'll find out how you self-identify. Based on your analysis, you'll understand your self-concept and how you perceive yourself. How you see yourself is more important than how others see you, as it will determine your outcomes long before you even get to them. A healthy self-identity is essential to aligning with our Nomadic Soul mission.

Instructions: In your journal, note any thoughts, ideas, and breakthroughs that you receive while reading through this section. Writing your ideas down will give structure and clarity to your thoughts. Do not rush this process, and take as long as you need.

Self-analysis is a reflective process that requires time and space for genuine answers to emerge.

Some of these may be a stretch for you and feel outside your comfort zone. Even if you haven't ever considered these questions before, stick with the process and trust it. You'll be surprised by the untapped truths about yourself that you might uncover.

Be willing to look deep within and ask, *What makes me ME?* What makes you unique and special? There are no right or wrong answers. Enjoy getting to know yourself better and using that knowledge to create a more fulfilling life that aligns with the path of your Nomadic Soul.

Part 1: Identify your core inner traits

Know thyself. There is profound truth in Socrates's words. Self-knowledge is the foundation of self-esteem because it won't be easy to find your way without it.

Throughout our lives, we'll encounter countless paths to choose from, and the only way to decipher what's right for us is by knowing ourselves. To do this, we need clarity around the fundamental traits that make up our identity, such as the following:

- **Core character traits:**
    - **Values**—Your judgment of what is important in your life (*example: freedom*).
    - **Ethics**—Moral principles or rules in relationship to what is and is not acceptable to you (*example: I have to be honest in all my dealings*).

  - **Personal standards**—Rules of behavior that you set for yourself (*example: I'm willing to work as many hours as possible to achieve a goal*).
  - **Beliefs**—The feeling of being certain that something exists or is true about yourself or the world (*example: I can do anything I set my heart on*).
- **Temperament**—Your personal dispositions, emotional responses, and habitual inclinations (*example: melancholic*).
- **Personal narrative of your life story thus far**—The perception you have of the events in your life and the causes you attribute to them (*example: I've lived a rags-to-riches story*).
- **Interests/hobbies/passions**—The things that excite, motivate, and drive you (*example: painting*).
- **Natural abilities and talents**—The things you can do better and more easily than most people (*example: negotiation and diplomacy*).
- **Perceived flaws and shadow traits**—The parts of you that you think get in the way of your happiness and success and that may cause you shame (*example: victim mentality*).

Journaling questions: Describe each core character trait and how it manifests in your identity and the choices you make. How aware are you of each trait's impact on you? Have you changed over the years? Are you happy with where your core traits are leading you? Are they aligned with your goals and vision for your life? Write your responses to each of these in your journal.

Part 2: Identify the identity shapers in your life

In addition to your core inner traits, there are several *identity shapers* that add layers to your persona. Below are the four general categories of identity shapers that impact you:

- **Official/inherited**—Identity influencers you inherited by birth and the circumstances you were born into.
- **Professional**—Identity influencers that you've earned through your profession and vocation.
- **Social or collective identity**—Identity influencers you've gained through your association with groups you belong to.
- **Aspirations or hobbies**—Identity influencers connected to things you're passionate about that you like to do in your spare time.

Here is a comprehensive list of common identity shapers:

- Generational traits
- Birth order traits
- Family history and customs
- Family members and relatives
- Country of origin
- Passport/national identity
- Physical appearance
- Age
- Sexual orientation and preference
- Gender identity
- Race and ethnicity
- Cultural and ethnic background

- Titles, class, and status symbols
- Wealth and income level
- Significant other/partner/spouse
- Friendships and acquaintances
- Children, stepchildren, nieces, nephews
- Professional titles and accomplishments
- Passions and interests
- Causes you support
- Political parties, religious and spiritual communities, and sports teams
- Formal education: schools, universities, trade school
- Role models and mentors
- Self-education: books, courses, podcasts, workshops, mentors, thought leaders
- Institutions and groups (examples: networking organizations, hobby groups, sports teams, religious and spiritual institutions, cults, influencers, celebrity idols, fraternities and sororities, political parties, alum affiliations, etc.)
- Lifestyle (examples: marathon runner, keto follower, yoga enthusiast, digital nomad, etc.)
- Health conditions (examples: dyslexia, cancer survivor, addiction survivor, disabled, etc.)

Journaling questions: Which of the following identity shapers have played a significant role in your self-concept? To what extent have they affected your choices? How have they shown up in your life? Would you like to change how much power they have in defining who you are? Why is that important to you?

Part 3: Identify the blocks that prevent you from becoming an authentic person

Like clouds that prevent the sun from shining, identity blockers prevent us from shining our light into the world.

Here are some common identity blockers:

- Fear of vulnerability/rejection/criticism from peers, parents, family, and society
- Low self-esteem/self-belief
- Trauma or unresolved pain
- Stress, worry, and anxiety
- Health conditions and low energy levels
- People pleasing
- Fear of failure
- Systemic challenges that limit our freedom and options
- Dysfunctional/codependent relationships

Journaling questions: Do any of these identity blockers get in the way of you being your authentic self? To what extent do they inhibit you? Were there any past experiences that caused you to feel this way? What are some steps that you can take to begin overcoming them? What types of resources and support do you need to remove or reduce the impact of these blocks?

Step 2: Getting feedback from others

Now that you have a clearer idea about your self-concept, the next step is to get insight into what you look like from the outside world's perspective. A fundamental practice of successful people is getting others' feedback regularly. This is an important part of our growth and progress because we all have blind spots. Often, we are unaware of the tendencies or qualities that neutral, unbiased observers notice about us. When we get feedback from others, we create opportunities to work on our blind spots.

To get the most from this exercise, it's important to select people who you believe will give you a balanced and unbiased perspective, offering positive and constructive advice. The pool may include family members, friends, acquaintances, coworkers, mentors, or anyone else you think would be able to provide you with valuable feedback. Schedule time to speak with them either over the phone or in person, and ask them the following questions:

1. What are some words you would use to describe me and why?
2. Was your first impression of me accurate? How can I give a more accurate picture of who I am?
3. What do you believe are my strengths and unique traits?
4. What are some areas that I can improve on? Do you have any suggestions?

After completing all your interviews, process the information you have received from others and make it actionable by identifying the areas you would like to improve or accentuate and creating a plan and strategy. For example, if you want to develop more patience, you can incorporate a mindfulness practice in your daily life and practice affirmations whenever you find yourself becoming restless.

Journaling questions: Here are some journaling questions to consider responding to: What changes would you like to make based on the suggestions that you received? How closely do others' perceptions of you match your self-perception? How did receiving feedback from others make you feel? Were there any specific responses that triggered you? Why?

Important note:

1. During this process, ensure that you allow others to speak and avoid interrupting them.
2. If they say something that you do not like, don't hold it against them. Remember, they are only giving you honest feedback that will help you develop and grow.
3. If you feel triggered in the conversation, take a few deep breaths, and remember that no one is perfect. Pat yourself on the back for being courageous enough to hear the truth.

Being objective, without personalizing feedback, is the only way to become comfortable with receiving feedback from others. Be sure to schedule feedback sessions at least once a year to monitor your development and growth as you evolve.

Step 3: Develop authenticity habits and practices

The path to crafting and maintaining an authentic identity is challenging. There will always be temptation to sway you away from your path, especially when you are under the influence of others or if you're placed in situations with high pressure and stress. For this reason, you need to develop a daily authenticity practice to keep you steady and focused on the path of your Nomadic Soul.

Here are nine authenticity habits and practices to incorporate into your life:

1. Develop personal standards. Your standards form the bedrock of your identity. They are essentially your rule book for living. Standards are your signature brand, representing the essence of who you are in both your career and your personal life. They represent the quirks and characteristics that make you the unique person you are. People are less likely to overstep your boundaries and mistreat you when you have standards. We teach people how to treat us, and when we communicate our standards to others, they'll know where you draw the line and act accordingly.

Individuals who command a high level of respect from others are admired and treated with dignity. When we take the time to define standards that are grounded in self-knowledge, we increase our chances of manifesting a fulfilling life. Your career, relationships, and personal prosperity will reflect what you believe to be true about yourself and the rest of the world.

Here are some examples of personal standards:

- I will not knowingly hurt or hinder another human being in my pursuit of growth.
- I will not knowingly break any laws.
- I will stick with my moral code no matter what circumstances I face.
- I will endeavor to make a positive contribution to society and give back to the world.
- I will not be jealous of others and choose to celebrate their successes.
- I will question the long-term ramifications of what I do.
- I will treat my body with respect by caring for and nurturing it.

2. Prioritize "me time" during your day. Just as you spend time with loved ones to strengthen your bond, you need to spend quality time with yourself to get to know you better. During these solitary sessions, you can engage in soul-enhancing activities such as mindfulness practices, writing, prayer, and repeating mantras and affirmations. Through these practices you can forge and deepen your connection with your inner world. You could also use this time to revisit your list of goals, dreams, and the vision you have for your life. You can write these down on Post-it notes and stick them in a place where you can view them during your day. If you prefer something more visual, you could create a vision board filled with images that elicit a sense of hope and positive anticipation about future possibilities.

3. Create a plan of action to deal with identity blockers. Look at your list of identity blockers and create an action plan to improve those areas.

Here are some ideas to get you started:

- Working with a coach or therapist
- Reading books
- Taking a workshop or course
- Retraining your thinking patterns
- Participating in a support group
- Reading relevant articles
- Listening to podcasts

Experiment with these methods to find the ones that work best for you. Stay consistent, as it takes some time to shift patterns that have been ingrained in you for a considerable period.

4. Let your life reflect your authenticity. Work toward creating a lifestyle and environment that centers on your authenticity. This can include the design of your home, how you raise your children, your hobbies and passions, your career choices, the causes you support, and the kinds of people you surround yourself with. Your life should be a representation of what you stand for and what you're all about. Through your lifestyle, you can demonstrate that you "walk your talk."

5. Make personal development a priority. Our identity is like a canvas that we continually enhance with hues and textures. It's a painting that will never be finished, a constant work in progress. Your objective as a Nomadic Soul is to explore your full potential by doing things that will help you grow, evolve, and expand. We can learn about ourselves from every experience we have if we allow time to reflect on them later. There are plenty of self-discovery tools you can use to increase your self-knowledge, from personality tests such as Myers-Briggs Type Indicator (MBTI) to metaphysical tools such as astrology. Each experience will reveal another layer of your persona that adds more dimension to self-understanding.

6. Dress and act the part. When people meet you, what kind of vibe do you think they pick up from you? Impression management is crucial in both your personal and your professional life. You'll only be able to attract the right people and opportunities if you do it right. You should think of yourself as a brand. Package yourself accordingly from your clothes to how you speak and behave. This isn't to say that you should develop a contrived persona just to please others and get ahead in life. Your outward appearance should be a genuine portrayal of who you are and what you stand for, packaged in the best possible way. If appearances are an important part of what you do for a living, you might want to consider working with an image consultant and a personal branding expert to craft the right image.

7. Don't be afraid to show your humanness to others. No one likes to be around a little miss (or mister) perfect. Plenty of research shows that we tend to like those who are fallible. If we're wearing a mask of perfection, we're not going to get the results we want from our interactions. To build trust with others, we must allow ourselves to be vulnerable. When we're willing to admit our mistakes, try something new, or ask for help and feedback from others, we show our humanity. This can put people at ease, making them more likely to open up to us. When used appropriately, vulnerability is not a flaw but a doorway that opens opportunities for meaningful and authentic connections based on trust.

8. Find authenticity buddies. It's always more fun to make changes in our lives when we have a community of people aspiring to do the same. An authenticity buddy is not only someone who can hold you accountable for staying on course but also someone that you can rely on for support and comfort. They are the soft cushions that you can fall back on whenever you're feeling vulnerable during the ups and downs of your life and when you are faced with temptations that can take you off course.

9. Be open to experimenting and reinventing yourself. You are a living, breathing entity—one that requires constant attention and updates. Having a core essence that you stay true to doesn't mean you have to remain stagnant and not change things up occasionally. Until recently, most people accepted the identities they were born and raised with. Their identity labels—religion, gender, sexuality, occupation, class, and community—were mainly fixed. Today all those can fluctuate. Many people change at least one or several of them. It's not uncommon to meet people who convert to another religion or use different pronouns. Not all changes in identity have to be drastic. In our fast-changing world, we may be drawn to experimenting and reinventing ourselves.

A famous person who's done this well is Madonna. Throughout her career, she has experimented with different looks, sounds, and styles, but her fundamental essence has not changed in the process. While her most recent looks and statements have been controversial, she remains an icon based on her past achievements and the longevity of her career.

Evolving yourself like Madonna did will help you stay relevant to the times and relatable to others. You might also discover fragments of yourself that you were not aware of in the past. Constantly evolving will add more dimension and nuance to your personality. Besides changing our appearance, we can continue to upgrade ourselves through education, learning new skills, traveling, networking with different kinds of people, and exposing ourselves to different environments.

Developing Your Identity Is a Lifelong Quest

Developing a deeper understanding of who we are is a lifelong quest. We are in a constant state of becoming, an endless state of evolution in which we are constantly changing, shifting, pivoting and becoming more (and less) at the same time. As we go through life, we gain more insight into our character and grow more comfortable in our own skin. The person we knew ourselves to be in our twenties transforms into a new person as we age. Be open to your personal evolution with each passing year, but stay anchored in the essence of your authentic identity.

No matter what you choose to integrate into your persona (or remove) along the way, always stay in integrity with your core ethics. "Being true to yourself" is not just a cliché. It's a practice and a state of awareness we need to cultivate actively. There are plenty of tools, theories, and techniques that you can look into as you continue this journey into self. The framework in this chapter will help you build the foundation that you need to unveil the magnificence of your Nomadic Soul.

NEED #2

Explore and Learn

Curiosity is a fundamental characteristic of human nature. All of us are born curious because curiosity is encoded in our DNA. Our drive to explore the unknown, push boundaries, and discover new worlds leads us to scientific, social, and technological breakthroughs and will for many years to come.

Case Study: Walt Disney (1901–1966)

"When you're curious, you find lots of interesting things to do."

An intense curiosity transformed Walt Disney from a bankrupt high school dropout to a pioneer in the American animation industry. Undoubtedly, there were several vital ingredients that made him an unprecedented success, but what fueled him was his curiosity. From his humble beginnings as a young boy in Kansas to his last days as a thriving entrepreneur in animation and entertainment, Walt displayed an insatiable desire to learn, explore possibilities, and put his knowledge to use.

Born in Chicago in 1901, Walter Elias Disney was the fourth son of Elias Disney, a carpenter, farmer, and building contractor, and Flora Call, a public school teacher. The Disneys were not a wealthy family and moved several times out of economic necessity. However, Walt's humble background didn't hold him back from pursuing his interests and reaching his potential.

When Walt was four, the family relocated to a farmhouse close to Marceline, Missouri, a small midwestern town. There he began his schooling. Encouraged by a favorite aunt, he had his first taste of creativity and started showing a talent for drawing with crayons and painting with watercolors. The family didn't stay too long in Marceline, however. Walt's father decided to quit his farming venture to search for other entrepreneurial adventures, uprooting the family and moving them to Kansas City. After the move, Walt's love for drawing grew. While attending school, Walt took Saturday drawing classes at the Kansas City Art Institute, as well as a correspondence course in cartooning.

After their stint in Kansas City, the Disneys were on the move again. They returned to Chicago, where Walt took photographs and made drawings for his school's newspaper while also studying cartooning. He hoped to get a job as a newspaper cartoonist after finishing his studies and continued to make slow, steady progress toward his dream. While his father couldn't understand his son's ambition to be a cartoonist, he still agreed to pay for Walt's art classes at the Chicago Academy of Fine Arts. Family meant everything to both father and son. Having the freedom to explore his interests at a young age amplified Walt's efforts to forge his unusual path.

But as World War I broke out, he had to put his dreams on hold to serve his country. Lying about his age, he volunteered to work as an ambulance driver in Germany and France for the American Red Cross. But even while serving, Walt could not contain his creative urges. True to form, Walt covered his ambulance with his drawings and cartoons.

After the war, he returned to Kansas City. While reintegrating himself into society, Walt was able to find sporadic employment as a draftsman and inker in commercial art studios in the city. He wasn't an instant success. Walt was once fired by the *Kansas City Star* for what his editor deemed his lack of imagination. The man who created Mickey Mouse, Goofy, and Donald Duck was accused of not having good ideas! But even Walt himself didn't think so highly of his talent, once recalling, "Now, to tell you the truth, I was never a good artist. I was never satisfied with what I did, but it was a means to an end." Despite his perceived lack of artistic talent and the many rejections he received in the early years, Walt persevered. During one of his gigs, he met Ub Iwerks, a young and enthusiastic artist who shared the same curiosity and ambition as he did. This was a fateful meeting, as his collaboration with Iwerks played an integral part in Walt's early success.

Unhappy with the pace of their career growth, Walt and Iwerks decided to establish a small studio of their own in 1922. It was in this studio that they made their first productions together. With a hand-me-down camera, they created one- and two-minute animations that advertised films for distribution to local movie theaters. They also produced a cartoon series called *Laugh-O-Grams*. And they created the pilot for a string of seven-minute fairy tales that combined live action and animation, which they called *Alice in Cartoonland*.

But while it seemed that the two friends were heading toward an imminent breakout, it wasn't long before a New York film distributor took advantage of them. The distributor cheated the duo out of their earnings, causing them to fall short of the funding needed to run their business. Walt was forced to file for bankruptcy. This was Walt's first real lesson in the ups and downs of entrepreneurship. Undeterred, he quickly found his stride again. He decided to try something else, leaving his partnership with Iwerks and moving to California with just forty dollars in his pocket.

Once in California, he ventured into cinematography. The unanticipated success of the *Alice in Cartoonland* series convinced him to open shop in Hollywood with his brother Roy Disney, who would end up being his lifelong business partner. Walt resumed producing *Alice in Cartoonland*, with his brother as business manager. He persuaded Iwerks to join him again to assist with drawing the cartoons. Together, they invented a character called Oswald the Lucky Rabbit. They also got a contract to distribute the films, taking their business venture to the next level of development. However, Walt suffered another setback when trying to negotiate a fee increase for producing the series. Unable to get the increase and unable to take Oswald with him because Universal Pictures owned the rights to the character, Walt walked out and brought Iwerks with him. Once again, they needed to reinvent themselves.

In 1927, Walt and Iwerks began experimenting with a new character—a cheerful and mischievous mouse called Mickey. Initially, they had planned for just two shorts: *Plane Crazy* and *The Gallopin' Gaucho*. These shorts would introduce Mickey Mouse to the public, who eventually came to love and embrace the character.

"He popped out of my mind onto a drawing pad twenty years ago on a train ride from Manhattan to Hollywood at a time when the business fortunes of my brother Roy and myself were at lowest ebb, and disaster seemed right around the corner," Walt wrote in a 1948 essay titled "What Mickey Means to Me." Walt was never one to let a setback stop him from moving forward. Like many curious people, he continued to dig deep into his creative reserves until he struck gold.

Upon the release of *The Jazz Singer*, the first feature-length motion picture with a synchronized recorded music score and lip-synched singing and speech, Walt was eager to incorporate the new technology into his animated shorts. They produced a third Mickey Mouse short that included voices and music and titled it *Steamboat Willie*. Their efforts paid off, and *Steamboat Willie* was a resounding success when it was released in 1928.

Always on the lookout for new trends and innovations, Walt fully expressed the inquisitive side of his Nomadic Soul throughout his journey. His curiosity propelled him to spearhead breakthroughs in animation and entertainment. This was a remarkable feat, considering that, at the start of his career, he knew next to nothing about the technology and artistry that went into creating cartoons. He educated himself by experimenting, observing others, and engaging in trial and error until he felt satisfied with the results.

Even though Walt dropped out of high school when he was sixteen, he never stopped learning. Whenever an idea struck him, he would study every aspect of it, looking at it from every angle possible. He would dive deeper into a subject by consulting experts, reading books, observing everything around him, and synthesizing it. He would then transmute his insights into viable plans and ideas that he could bring to life. People who knew him said that he was always alert and hardly ever missed a beat when it came to his projects.

When producing a film in color became a possibility, Walt was eager to try it, and he did it with *Flowers and Trees*, which became the first cartoon to win an Academy Award. Lillian Disney told historian Richard Hubler that her husband wanted to try color because "it was new." She recalled, "He just wanted to do it. He was always interested in new things. I used to go along with him at night. We would go from theater to theater . . . He was just absorbing what everyone made—searching for new ideas and for new techniques to adapt."

Not long after, Walt was inspired to take on another challenge on the heels of his remarkable success. He explored the possibility of making the world's first full-length animated movie. His animators were initially taken aback at the thought of drawing an eighty-minute film, but they were intrigued by Walt's idea and his courage to cross boundaries. "He was doing something no other studio had ever attempted," art director Ken Anderson later said, "but his excitement over *Snow White and the Seven Dwarfs* inspired us all."

Animator Ollie Johnston said, "It took guts to do what Walt did." Even though the rest of the Hollywood film industry was skeptical—going so far as to refer to *Snow White* as "Disney's Folly" behind closed doors—Walt pressed on with his vision. His innate curiosity gave him insight into opportunities that others couldn't see and the confidence to pursue what others thought was too risky. He saw the possibilities for growth in the hurdles that needed to be overcome—like funding his vision for *Snow White*. The movie's production ended up costing ten times more than Walt's studio anticipated. Walt even had to bet on his assets, such as his house, against production costs to finish the film. Despite the financial hurdles, *Snow White and the Seven Dwarfs* was an instant success when it was released on December 21, 1937. Its success was phenomenal, as the movie went on to gross a whopping $8 million ($139 million today).

The people who had the privilege to work with Walt said that he was never satisfied with repeating his past successes and was quick to move on to the next challenge. He was constantly searching for ways to break new ground and accomplish things that were never done before. This drive to keep moving forward made him a pioneer in his field. He consistently demonstrated this over the course of his career as he created the first cartoon with sound, the first full-length animated movie, and the first large-scale theme park. He summed up his attitude toward new challenges when he famously said, "It's kind of fun to do the impossible!"

His passion for growing and continually adding value to the viewer's experience saw him become one of the first people to use television as a medium for entertainment, producing hit TV shows like *Zorro* and *Davy Crockett*, *The Mickey Mouse Club*, and *Walt Disney's Wonderful World of Color*, which he used to promote his new theme park.

By this time, Walt Disney Studios had become a well-oiled, self-sustaining machine, and Walt was ready to spearhead another breakthrough project. In 1964, Walt produced the motion picture *Mary Poppins*. It combined live action and animation and received widespread critical acclaim and thirteen Academy Award nominations. It was another innovative, successful production that Walt was personally involved with.

During that period, Walt oversaw the release of over one hundred feature films by his studio. Even while he was at his creative peak, he continued to learn and educate himself on the newest technologies and explore different storytelling formats. So deep was his love and respect for learning that he insisted that his employees get regular training and education themselves. Animators were sent to art classes to improve their skills, and if Walt had enough money, he would hire art teachers to give lessons in the studio. During the planning phase of Disneyland, he sent Imagineers—a term he coined for people who created and implemented the highly innovative technology at his theme park—to carnivals and amusement parks so they could understand the complaints and grievances of visitors. They would use this knowledge to enhance the visitor experience in Disneyland.

Despite the growth and success of Walt Disney Animation Studios, Walt's desire to explore the realms of family entertainment did not cease. For many years, he incubated the idea of opening an amusement park, an idea that came to him during outings with his daughters to Griffith Park in Los Angeles on Saturday mornings: "Well, it came about when my daughters were very young, and Saturday was always Daddy's Day with the two daughters . . . I'd take them to the merry-go-round . . . and as I'd sit there while they rode the merry-go-round and did all these things—sit on a bench, you know, eating peanuts—I felt that there should be something built, some kind of amusement enterprise built, where the parents and the children could have fun together." A family trip to the Tivoli Gardens in Copenhagen further solidified his vision to create something similar in the United States.

Disneyland didn't go from idea to reality overnight. Walt said, "It took many years. It was a whole period of maybe fifteen years developing. I started with many ideas, threw them away, started again, and eventually it evolved into what you see today as Disneyland." Walt had no qualms about throwing out ideas that weren't working. He set his ego aside and used his passion to sustain himself as he worked hard to ensure Disneyland would be more than just a place families could spend a few hours. He wanted the park to be a place "where dreams come true."

In the summer of 1955, Walt opened the $17 million Disneyland theme park in Anaheim, California. Despite a chaotic opening day that saw the distribution of over a thousand counterfeit invitations and technical issues in the park, Disneyland became a renowned tourist attraction. Within a short period of time, the park had made its investment back tenfold and was entertaining tourists from all over the world. Walt took great pride in his creation, and he wanted to continue to build on its success. "Disneyland will never be completed," he once said. "It will continue to grow as long as there is imagination left in the world."

A few years after opening Disneyland, Walt was already looking to expand his amusement park enterprise. He began plans for a new theme park, this one a futuristic urban city in Florida called EPCOT, which stands for Experimental Prototype Community of Tomorrow. But while the project was under construction, Walt was diagnosed with lung cancer. And in a few short months, on December 15, 1966, Walt Disney died at the age of sixty-five. After his death, Walt's brother and longtime business partner, Roy Disney, carried on with the plan and finished the Florida theme park. It opened in 1971 under the name "Walt Disney World."

A pioneer in the American animation industry, Walt Disney was an entrepreneur, animator, voice actor, and producer who won millions of hearts. His evergreen creations are a testament to his dream of bringing the joy of family entertainment to the masses. Through the crucible of his vivid imagination, he created a diverse entertainment empire that continues to inspire Disney lovers around the world and will no doubt continue to do so for generations.

Walt Disney's legacy inspires us to open up our minds and explore the unknown. No matter how much wealth he accumulated, he always knew that real wealth was found in his pursuit of knowledge. Despite coming from a family of modest means, he found ways to pursue his interests, whether it was through training or experience. Even at the height of his success, he wanted to learn about new technologies and topics that could take his artistry and business to the next level. Walt may have dropped out of high school, but he remained the eternal student who applied his knowledge to improve the world, making him an exemplary Nomadic Soul. He emphasized his love for learning when he said, "There is more treasure in books than in all the pirates' loot in Treasure Island."

Understanding Our Need: The Gift of Curiosity

Human Beings Are Naturally Curious

Curiosity is a fundamental human trait. It enabled our species to evolve and survive environmental threats such as extreme climatic conditions, dangerous predatory animals, and the other species that were competing for resources.

When humans first appeared on Earth some 250,000 to 400,000 years ago, several human species existed, such as Homo Neanderthals, Home erectus, Homo habilis, and others. However, only the Homo sapiens survived, while the others perished.

Anthropologists believe that Homo sapiens were able to stand the test of time because of their survival instincts and unique traits that set them apart from their contemporaries. One of those traits is our ability to quickly adapt to new environments. Second to this is our propensity to question things and follow our innate curiosity.

The roots of our curiosity can be linked to a species trait known as neoteny. This evolutionary theory refers to the "retention of juvenile characteristics." Neoteny has given humans this child-like capacity more than other mammals. Physical manifestations include being relatively hairless and having a large brain relative to body size. The behavioral manifestation of neoteny includes our playfulness and curiosity.

Neoteny has worked well for our species and opened us up to new ways of thinking and doing things. As we've evolved over the centuries, we've continued to make great strides because of our adaptability and curiosity. All major discoveries and artistic endeavors took root from the seeds of curiosity. Our civilization progressed because of the likes of Galileo Galilei, Christopher Columbus, Marie Curie, Thomas Edison, Edward Bouchet, Isaac Newton, and countless others. These figures weren't afraid to ask the important questions: *Why? How? What?*

Our thirst for knowledge is not only a product of our natural impulses but also a result of how our brain is structured. Based on neuroimaging studies done by scientists, the same reward system in the brain that makes acts such as eating and lovemaking pleasurable also makes information seeking intrinsically satisfying.

Just like consuming food and procreation, accumulating knowledge is critical to our survival based on nature's parameters. Primates, such as humans, are informavores—creatures that seek and digest information. Just as carnivores hunt and consume meat, we hunger for knowledge because of how it lights up the pleasure centers in our brain and makes us feel good.

Where Curiosity Has Taken Us

Necessity is the mother of invention, and curiosity constantly prods us to know more than we already do. Hundreds of years ago, humans created fire by smashing rocks together. The fire caught on dry leaves and branches, and we used it to prepare animal game. It's curiosity that gave us life. We became the ultimate learning machines because of our evolutionary journey. With a healthy dose of curiosity, we could take full advantage of this learning ability.

People never allowed themselves to be bound by physical limitations. We are not as strong as the lion, nor do we weigh as much as the elephant. We cannot swim the lengths of the seas, nor can we fly with the birds of the sky. However, we have tamed the lion and made friends with the elephant. We have built ships that have crossed the Atlantic. We have built planes and flown over the surface of the earth. Our curiosity has brought us to a better place than we were three hundred years ago. By being curious, we can see a world filled with new possibilities normally invisible to others. Hidden behind the surface of everyday life, these new ways of living and being can be discovered only by those with a curious mind who are willing to look beyond the traditional confines the rest of the world subjects itself to.

Our curiosity is the reason we have set up school systems. We have gone to great lengths to understand animals and plants, viruses, germs, and plankton. We have gazed upon twinkling celestial bodies that are too small to be seen by naked eyes. We determined the laws of physics and attempted to break these laws. One of these laws states that what goes up must come down—gravitational pull. And yet we have gone up high above the stratosphere.

On May 25, 1961, President John F. Kennedy announced in a speech before both houses of Congress the goal of sending an American to the moon and bringing him back home safely. It was an ambitious goal born out of pure curiosity. In Kennedy's speech on September 12, 1962, he said that they were setting sail on this new sea because "there is new knowledge to be gained, and new rights to be won, and they must be won and used for the progress of all people."

No financial reward was attached to sending a man to the moon. Still, NASA took the mission upon itself and made it a possibility. It was an emotional endeavor, and they achieved it nine years later—right before the decade's end. Kennedy believed the challenge would "serve to organize and measure the best of our energies and skills."

Humans did not create the seas, yet we know an almost exact percentage of the amount of water on Earth. We know the components of the human body and cells. We divided the atom into proton, neutron, and electron and showed that there are particles even smaller than these. We thought about objects moving at the speed of light and created the bullet train. Over a century before trains could move at such unbelievable speeds, scientists had dreamed about and worked on the calculations of these trains.

Curiosity has allowed humans to find the cure to deadly diseases. Penicillin, one of the world's first antibiotics, was born from a curious mind. Alexander Fleming made the discovery after examining mold that had developed on an accidentally contaminated staphylococcus culture that he left behind while on a two-week vacation. Driven to confirm his prognosis, he allowed it to grow for a few more weeks to verify that this mold could effectively prevent the staphylococci bacteria's growth. Other medical breakthroughs include improvements to our treatments for malaria, typhoid, breast cancer, leukemia, depression, gonorrhea, and hundreds more once-life-threatening conditions. In 2020, scientists around the world banded together to find a vaccine to immunize people against the deadly coronavirus and eventually succeeded.

The Information Age has led to global connectivity. Online marketplaces give us a platform through which we can interact safely with people we have never seen. Google is the brainchild of two zealous tech-heads who decided to aggregate the information about everything under the sun online. Business magnate Elon Musk founded SpaceX, a private spaceflight company that sends satellites and people to space with the hope that it will lead to future crewed Mars missions and even regular space travel. Flying to outer space would become accessible to anyone willing to be jetted outside of Earth—not just astronauts.

Curiosity is the light that envelops the darkness. It is boundless because the human mind never rests. It has taken us from the Stone Age to the Information Age. Our drive to explore the unknown, push the boundaries, and discover new worlds will continue to lead us to scientific, social, and technological breakthroughs. Our insatiable desire to learn and grow and challenge the limits of what we know has advanced our civilization in remarkable ways, and it will continue to do so for years to come if we follow the beacon of curiosity.

The Ways We Limit Our Drive to Explore and Learn

Limiting your ability to explore and learn stunts your growth and evolution as a Nomadic Soul. You inhibit your potential to master the areas in which you have a natural talent. Seeds of opportunities remain untouched, and you live a life of mediocrity, not realizing your gifts. Others lose because they don't get to receive the unique offerings only you can give. A deprivation of knowledge leads to ignorance and unhealthy attitudes that won't serve us or those around us. There are three ways that we block learning opportunities—fear, avoidance, and pride.

Learning Block 1: Fear

Humans are often afraid of the unknown. We're wired to stick with what's familiar because we perceive it as safe. A child burned by a candle flame learns from the experience and may never go near a lit candle again. Fear is an evolutionary response that protects us, but when it's unfounded, it paralyzes us. We become afraid to step outside our comfort zone.

During specific eras, such as Medieval Europe, education was not widely accessible. Formal schooling was reserved for the wealthy or those who studied in monasteries to become monks. People in those eras found no value in investing in educational pursuits, often proselytizing that it could lead to dangerous thoughts that threatened the traditions they clung to.

Knowledge that did not align with the prevailing doctrine was seen as disrupting the status quo. Those who pursued such subjects were considered heathens and heretics. There were only certain periods when the church's authority on education was challenged, such as during the Renaissance. During this time, an interest in intellectual, cultural, and scientific exploration flourished and gained the support of wealthy patrons, thus diminishing the hold of religious institutions.

Fear can also seduce us into using our curiosity for the wrong purposes. For instance, Japan's nuclear-powered plants provide power to more than half of the country's citizens. Yet the US military used that same nuclear power to create and drop an atomic bomb that claimed the lives of over a million people in Hiroshima and Nagasaki in 1945. Our intention for learning must always come from a place of compassion, knowing that it could somehow benefit the lives of others.

Learning Block 2: Avoidance

Learning is considered a tedious activity by some individuals. Tried and tested ways of doing things are less demanding on the brain. Consuming new information and adopting new behaviors require more focus, energy, and concentration, which can be a chore—especially if learning does not lead to material gain or praise. After a hard day's work, most professionals prefer to veg out on the couch and watch their favorite Netflix show or a sports game than to read a book or attend an informative lecture. After using up all their mental reserves during the day, they want instant gratification. They want to relax and engage in easier pursuits.

However, opening that book or attending that lecture can stimulate us and expand our mind's capacity. In opening ourselves up to learning opportunities, we realize the powerhouse that our minds are. When we choose topics that interest us, learning can actually be fun. If you have forgotten what that feels like, look into the eyes of any kid, and you will be able to see their genuine sense of wonder and their relentless efforts to get answers to the things they don't understand. That childlike curiosity lives in you too.

Learning Block 3: Pride

Pride also impedes our capacity to learn. Some people believe that they know enough and that active learning stops once they're done with school or university. After that, it's time to work, raise a family, and pay the bills. This attitude builds a wall around a person's mind and holds them back from seeking learning opportunities. Ancient Greek philosopher Plato, considered one of the greatest thinkers in history, towered over his contemporaries because of his humility. He said, "I am the wisest man alive, for I know one thing, and that is that I know nothing." Plato knew that there is always a higher plane that we should strive for. The curious mind knows that it knows nothing and seeks to learn more every single day.

The Global Education Crisis

Our drive to explore and learn is also influenced by macro factors affecting the collective. As Nomadic Souls, it's important to be aware of the places in the world where this need is largely unmet. Gary Zukav wrote, "What is in one is in the whole, and therefore, ultimately, each soul is responsible for the world." When it comes to fostering a love for learning on a global scale, we face challenges such as the need for proper infrastructure and living conditions. Poverty and hunger diminish any trace of curiosity that a person might have. Lack of good schools, where the first seeds of interest are usually planted and nurtured, are unavailable in many poor neighborhoods and developing nations around the world.

Education allows students to broaden their horizons and teaches them to think critically. Through education, they can create an exploratory approach to living. Sadly, millions of adults and children lack access to quality education for a number of reasons. Some aren't allowed to attend school because they're girls or because their families need them to work to support the family. Children who live in conflict zones often have limited access to education. Studies done by UNESCO show that fifty-nine million school-age kids are currently being denied an education, and sixty-five million don't have access to a secondary school.

Malala Yousafzai, one of the many victims who was shot by a Taliban hitman in Pakistan in 2012, is an advocate for women's education. In Malala's moving and impactful speech about the importance of equitable access to education, she encouraged world leaders to provide free and mandatory education to every child on the planet. She said, "We realized the importance of pens and books when we saw the guns. We realized the importance of light. We realized the importance of our voice when we are silenced."

She received a standing ovation at this point in her speech. She smiled as she continued on to say, "Let us pick up our books and our pens. They are our most powerful weapons. One child, one teacher, one book, and one pen can change the world. Education is the only solution to illiteracy, poverty, and terrorism."

Malala has become a major figure in the global discussion about education because of the wisdom that she has gleaned from her terrifying experiences with the Taliban in her community. Living under the pressure and subjugation of an extreme regime opened her eyes to the value of education and learning and their capacity to unlock human potential.

The global education crisis gives us yet another reason to work through any learning blocks within us. Once we overcome these blocks, we can use our knowledge to improve the conditions in the areas where education is scarce or isn't encouraged. Whether we choose to raise funds to send books to schools or to tutor a homeless child, we can contribute in our own unique way and make the world a better place, which is our ultimate goal as Nomadic Souls.

The Gift of Curiosity: How Being Curious Benefits Us

All of us are born curious. As children, we were exceptionally curious and had a deep love for learning new things. We weren't afraid to explore and ask questions incessantly until we were satisfied. Life was one grand adventure, and we were the protagonists, out to discover new territory every day. During this phase of our life, we were deeply in tune with the Curious and Pioneering Spirit Archetype of our Nomadic Soul—the part of us that loves to explore, innovate, and push boundaries.

Reconnecting with our curiosity is critical to our success. Our society has moved out of the industrial era and into the Information Age, where exploring new territories and coming up with innovative ideas can open doors, possibilities, and riches for us. Global wealth is no longer limited to aristocrats and the bourgeoisie but can be earned by entrepreneurs, artists, and tech-geniuses who follow their sparks of curiosity.

Staying curious can also kick our "happiness set point" up a few notches. In his book *Curious?: Discover the Missing Ingredient to a*

Fulfilling Life, author Todd Kashdan wrote, "Curious explorers are comfortable with the risks of taking on new challenges. Instead of trying desperately to explain and control their world, a curious explorer embraces uncertainty and sees life as an enjoyable quest to discover, learn, and grow."

Following our curiosity is an exciting prospect because we can never know where it will take us. It's like setting off on an expedition that can lead us to something wonderful. If we're tuned in, it can take us on a journey toward a greater understanding of who we are and what our purpose is. Walt Disney pointed this out when he famously said, "We keep moving forward, opening new doors, and doing new things, because we're curious and curiosity keeps leading us down new paths."

There's plenty of evidence to support the claim that curious people are some of the happiest and most content on the planet. These wide-eyed folks have a lot more fun than others, but they also experience several other surprising benefits.

They are more likely to stumble upon the right opportunities. Curious people have the drive and impetus to dig deep into a subject they love until they strike gold. They have the tenacity and patience to hang on long enough until the right opportunities come. Their curiosity gives them the insight to see new worlds and possibilities that aren't normally visible to others. They're willing to look beneath the surface of things and venture into the unknown. Unlike most people, they are comfortable with uncertainty, and instead of fearing the unknown, they are stimulated by it. They tend to stumble upon good fortune because they willingly step into new territory where valuable ideas and inspirations can be found.

They have a growth mindset, which leads to progress. Curious people are focused on the possibilities for growth versus the constraints in a situation. Whenever someone told Walt Disney that something could not be done or was a bad idea, whether it was doing the first feature-length cartoon (*Snow White* in 1939) or building a large-scale theme park for families (Disneyland), he always found a way to get it done and prove that person wrong. He was a bold risk taker with an active mind, who was always searching for solutions. Curious people like him are too focused on progress to worry about the limitations and negativity of naysayers. A learner's mindset is free from mental shackles.

They're hardly ever bored. If you've ever been around a curious person, you'll notice that they have an almost childlike disposition, always on the lookout for the latest news and happenings. To them, life is like a thrilling ride filled with a myriad of things that attract their attention—people to meet, things to learn, and new "toys" to play with. There's hardly a dull moment in their life with their active imaginations and their natural effervescence.

They're popular and well respected by others. Curious people often make exciting and engaging conversationalists with their knowledge and enthusiasm for life. They always have many unusual tidbits of information, anecdotes, and stories to share with others. They're also great listeners because of their genuine curiosity about other people. Their sincere interest in people is flattering to those who speak with them. It makes them likable because almost everyone enjoys spending time with them. A learner's mindset also reduces pride and ego. When you are in awe of the things you do not know, the things you know will begin to matter less than the things you want to know. You become more tolerant of others' differences and are more accepting of the differences in other people.

They understand life on a deeper level. It takes a reflective and inquiring mind to access the deeper dimensions of life. All religious, philosophical, and literary luminaries reached a state of enlightenment and had breakthroughs because they asked penetrating questions that revealed to them the hidden truths of life. They weren't distracted by superficial matters such as gossip or the latest scoop but were instead invested in worldly, intellectual, and spiritual matters that injected wisdom and meaning into their existence. Living in this state of inquiry creates an internal experience steeped in magic and wonder.

So don't be afraid to put on your explorer hat and seek out the mysterious and the unfamiliar. Following your curiosity doesn't take a massive effort—just a willingness to follow your impulses. In the next section, you'll learn about the nuts and bolts of developing your curiosity and increasing learning opportunities to help you move forward with specific goals that will spark your curiosity.

Albert Einstein summed up this truth when he said, "The important thing is not to stop questioning. Curiosity has its own reason for existing. It is enough if one tries merely to comprehend a little of this mystery every day. Never lose a holy curiosity." Read that book, take that course, ask questions, maintain an open mind, and stay humble in your pursuit of knowledge. And, most importantly, view learning as a fun activity.

Digging Deep: How to Bring Out Your Inner Explorer

How to Meet Our Need to Explore and Learn

In the Disney movie *Beauty and the Beast*, there is an impressive scene where the Beast surprises Belle with access to his enormous and grand library room. Each wall of the ceiling-high bookshelves is filled with hundreds and hundreds of books. Belle, a passionate reader, is ecstatic at the sight of the ocean of books presented to her. It was beyond her wildest dreams and something that she had not even conceived in her mind, having been used to the meager book selection in the archaic library in her village.

The modest bookstore in her town was a testament to the lack of interest that the town folk had in learning. They had little interest in immersing themselves in books and engaging their mind or imagination. They looked at inquisitive women like Belle with suspicion, considering her an outcast. Even though *Beauty and the Beast* is fictional, it does reflect the truths during those times. Provincial folks were mostly close-minded, and they preferred to ignore anything beyond their townships' confines that didn't align with their perception of the world. They were comfortable with the beliefs and customs they were accustomed to and didn't feel the need to question them.

Belle was a misfit in the rural countryside of nineteenth-century France, yet she would have fit right in if she lived in the twenty-first century, where knowledge is the primary currency. The saying is no longer "whoever has the gold makes the rules" but "whoever has the most knowledge makes the rules." The wealthiest and most successful people today are on a constant quest to learn and grow. Unlike in the past, the richest and most influential people in the world are no longer just those born with titles and hereditary wealth. The new rich are those who have honed their skills and developed specialized knowledge that enables them to build successful careers.

The secret to their success is their powerful drive and tenacity to evolve and expand their mind. More importantly, they are selective about the materials they want to learn and topics they want to spend their time on. They also tune out distractions that could sway them from their path. This form of discernment is essential in today's times, when we're flooded with data and information. Unlike our ancestors who faced information scarcity, we're now dealing with information overload.

Elon Musk, one of the wealthiest men in the world, was born with a high IQ. Although he made his name in tech innovations, when asked what advice he would give to young people today, he said, "I read a lot of books." When asked how he learned to build spaceships, he said that he read Russian books about astrodynamics and rocket propulsion. He also surrounded himself with people like Jim Cantrell, an aerospace consultant. According to Musk, if you want to succeed in life, improve your knowledge—that means read anything and everything about your field. His mother, Maye Musk, says he read two sets of encyclopedias at a very young age.

In the past, the average person had little or no access to educational resources. Today we're inundated with them, all available at our fingertips. Even in countries lacking access to quality education, people can source unlimited amounts of data on the internet via courses, e-books, videos, how-to articles, and podcasts, many of which are available for free. We can consume these information products on modern technological devices such as our sleek desktops, laptops, smartphones, and e-readers. However, our minds are trying to keep up with the fast pace of modern-day life, demands on our time, and technology overwhelm, all of which dampen our enthusiasm for learning and growth.

As a Nomadic Soul, you can connect to your natural love for learning and exploration by shielding yourself from this haphazard information flow. You must evaluate the quality of information you consume and how you consume it. Become mindful of your information diet because you have a limited mental bandwidth and time. Take in only those things that feed your curiosity and are relevant to your goals. When you're clear about your intention for learning, you can remove the stress and overwhelm. You cut out everything irrelevant and narrow it down to only those topics that appeal to you.

Let's explore a five-step process to bring out your inner explorer:

Step 1: Adopt the qualities of an explorer

Before you can become a natural explorer, you must adopt the mindset of one. You may already have some of these qualities, which you can deepen while cultivating other attributes that don't come naturally to you.

- **Curiosity and openness.** A person with an explorer mindset is curious and sees the world as one big school. Their minds are active because they are always learning and investigating subjects. They seek knowledge in the areas that interest them, but they are also open to gaining knowledge about other things. No matter where they are, they find something interesting to explore. No matter who they interact with, they try to learn from them, because they know everyone can teach them something new. Their life is filled with activities, and they always have interesting stories and facts to share with others.

Asking the right questions and looking at things from different angles opens up new avenues and possibilities for us to pursue. If we want to transform from average into excellent, we have to be willing to listen to what others have to say and try new things. Asking questions such as "How can I do better?" and "What do I need to improve on?" will propel our growth.

- **Humility.** An explorer has the emotional maturity and discernment to know that they don't know it all, no matter how intelligent and learned they are. They tame any traces of an inflated ego, grandiosity, and self-importance. They prevent it from dominating their consciousness and blocking them from learning new things. They have no qualms about asking questions and looking clueless in the process, because they understand that the path of learning requires a learner's mindset. It's okay to be a student outside the classroom.

- **Passion.** It's tough to stay committed to the learning process with all the distractions, noise, and choices available to us. Passion is that fire in your belly that will drive you to put in whatever work and time are necessary to achieve your goals. The love for learning and the determination to improve ourselves will supply the jet fuel you need to forge ahead in your learning journey.

- **Courage.** Most people are unwilling to take risks for a new learning adventure because of the possibility of failing and looking like an amateur. It takes a courageous and self-assured person to take that chance. This doesn't mean that explorers aren't afraid of failing. But they have learned how to manage fear while taking calculated steps toward their goals. The fact that you're putting yourself out there as a beginner who's willing to make mistakes along the way is a significant factor of success, regardless of the outcome.

- **Adaptable and flexible.** Learning is an adventure full of twists and turns. While it's important to maintain focus on your end goal for your knowledge, staying flexible about how and when you will reach your goal is essential. When you let go of your rigid outlook, you release yourself from the anxiety, worry, and disappointment that occur every time you hit a challenge.

  You're prepared for unforeseen changes and are willing to experiment and to find other routes. Some of the best practices to make it easier to go with the flow are mindfulness and deep breathing techniques, staying in the present moment, and having a sense of humor.

- **Creativity.** With all the learning resources out there, we have plenty of opportunities to be creative in our approach. What materials are you going to use? How are you going to fit creative activities into your schedule? How will you use what you learn to improve your life? An explorer's mind thinks outside the box, making connections that other people would not have thought of, which is the essence of creativity.

- **"No limit" thinking.** There are no limits to our capacity to learn and create. An explorer has a growth mindset, which leads to progress, focused on the possibilities versus the constraints in a situation. J. K. Rowling was a struggling single mother living on government welfare when she wrote the first *Harry Potter* book. She didn't let her circumstances fetter her imagination. Huddled in a café by a window, ordering coffee now and again, she concocted elaborate plots and captivating characters.

  Every explorer knows that at some point on their path to their goal, they will experience pushback. Novelist Steven Pressfield describes this resistance as an opposing universal force that keeps you from fulfilling your dreams. This resistance will make you believe that you are not good enough or don't have enough time or talent every time you attempt something new. The solution to overcoming this resistance is to realize that you're bigger and better than the things that hold you back. Remember that it's okay to slow down and take small steps, celebrating each victory. Taking a gradual, slow-and-steady approach makes those big dreams much more attainable.

- **Non-judgment.** As you embark on the learner's journey, you'll encounter belief systems, customs, mannerisms, and behaviors different from what you're used to. Someone with an explorer mindset strives to stay as neutral and open as possible while facing these different conditions. Instead of judging people and their ways of living that seem strange, labeling them based on what you consider the norm, appreciate difference for what it is. It's diversity that defines our beautiful planet. Your life is enriched when you're open to other perspectives and places.

- **Resourcefulness.** Time, energy, and money are limited resources. Yet this doesn't seem to be an issue for explorers because of their remarkable ability to maximize what they have been given. They have an "abundance mindset," which allows them to find and create opportunities for learning, regardless of their present circumstances. Whether they live in the African savannah or an Ivy League university dorm, they find a way to create learning opportunities.

- **Commitment.** Nomadic Souls make learning nonnegotiable. Whether they want to improve their relationships, build a successful business, or master a new skill, they stay committed to the learning process and gradually further their progress. For example, a person who's passionate about art and who feels committed to becoming an expert in their field will spend a sizable amount of money and number of hours immersing themselves in learning about all aspects of art. They'll investigate the history, techniques, styles, and genres; visit exhibitions and galleries; and network with other patrons and artists. Art becomes as natural as the blood that flows through their veins and becomes an integral part of their being.

Step 2: Determine your goals for learning

Most people get overwhelmed when they try to expand their minds and seek new knowledge because they do it haphazardly. Like anything else, you work best if you maintain a singular focus on what matters most and apply all your energy and effort there. When you have clear and purposeful goals relevant to your path, learning becomes a manageable, enjoyable conquest.

With this in mind, let's move to the next step in developing your Nomadic Soul's instinct for curiosity and exploration: setting your goals. At this stage, it's important to review the vision you hold for your life and what you would like to manifest in the long run. Ensure that your learning goals align with your personal and professional vision. Think about the key areas that you would like to develop and grow. What additional skills and knowledge do these goals require? Are there any existing knowledge gaps that you would like to fill? Is there a new subject or territory that you would like to explore?

To help you get started in this process, here are some examples of learning goals:

- Become a better conversationalist and improve my networking skills
- Quench my curiosity about a specific topic
- Stay informed about the world and broaden my horizons
- Develop new skills to progress in my career
- Learn and master a new skill
- Complete a particular project—a book, thesis, presentation, etc.
- Learn more about a cause that is important to me
- Explore the culture and history of a country I've wanted to visit

You can take your goal-setting strategy further by dividing your goals into short-term and long-term learning goals.

You can use the following writing prompts to further explore your goals. For each prompt, an example has been provided to illustrate how to use it.

My learning goal is . . . to become a better conversationalist

- *My intention for this learning goal is . . . to build my social network and seek mutually beneficial partnerships.*
- *Why is this important to me? . . . I can progress in my career and get insider industry knowledge.*
- *I want to achieve this learning goal in this time frame . . . one to two years.*

Step 3: Determine what kind of learner you are

Every person gravitates toward different learning styles and methods. Each of us has a dominant learning style that we're inclined to. We might have a mix of learning styles that appeal to us across various circumstances. No matter which types you prefer, knowing what kind of learner you are can help you tailor your self-education plan to suit your needs and maximize your ability to retain and apply information.

Look over this list and rank the learning styles that appeal to you the most. If you have a tough time figuring out your preferred style, think about how you liked to learn in school and college. Did you enjoy attending lectures (aural)? Did you like reading your textbooks (visual)? Did you enjoy doing experiments (physical)?

Here is a list of typical characteristics of each learner type. Your dominant learning style will be the one you identify with the most.

Signs that you are an aural learner (auditory-musical)

- You learn by hearing and listening.
- You understand and remember things you have heard.
- You store information by the way it sounds, and you have an easier time understanding spoken instructions instead of written ones.
- You often learn by reading aloud because you have to hear it or speak it to know it.
- People may think you are not paying attention, even though you hear and understand everything being said.

Signs that you are a visual learner (linguistic)

- You learn by reading or seeing pictures.
- You understand and remember things by sight.
- You can picture what you are learning in your head, and you grasp more by using primarily visual methods.
- You like to see what you are learning.
- You may have difficulty with spoken directions and may be easily distracted by sounds.
- You are attracted to color and stories rich in imagery.

Signs that you are a verbal learner (linguistic)

- You prefer using words, both in speech and writing.
- You have a good memory for the written or spoken word.
- You learn best from reading notes out loud, repeating and rephrasing words, and discussing concepts.
- You like activities where you can verbally express yourself, like presentations, interviews, debates, and speeches.

- You find it difficult to interpret a visual presentation of information.
- You may have a harder time with hand-eye coordination and visual-spatial tasks.

Signs that you are a physical learner (kinesthetic)

- You learn by touching and doing.
- You understand and remember things through physical movement.
- You are a hands-on learner who prefers to touch, move, build, or draw what you learn, and you tend to know better when some type of physical activity is involved.
- You like to take things apart and put things together, and you tend to find reasons to tinker or move around when you become bored.
- You can easily remember things that were done but may have difficulty remembering what you saw or heard.
- You often communicate by touching, and you appreciate physically expressed forms of encouragement, such as a pat on the back.

Step 4: Customize your information diet

Now you have set your learning goals and figured out your preferred learning styles, you have all the information you need to create a customized information diet that fuels your curiosity and leads you down exciting paths that may speak to your Nomadic Soul.

- **Prioritize your learning goals.** Examine your learning goals and rank their order of importance. Select one or two that you would like to dedicate yourself to in the near future. Some could be directly related to your goals, while others are things you want to learn just for fun.

- **Choose your preferred learning material.** We live in an age of information where we can access knowledge by clicking a button. You can now find information outside traditional print mediums such as books, audiobooks, newspapers, and magazines. The internet offers a vast repository of knowledge that you can easily access for little or no cost. Determine how you would like to consume information from the wide variety of information sources that are available to you. For example, if you are a visual learner, perhaps you would like more videos, presentations, and books. If you are an auditory learner, you prefer audiobooks and podcasts. Or you can consume a mix that can seamlessly fit into your lifestyle.

- **Create time in your schedule for learning sessions.** Most of us lead busy lives. It's essential that we carefully allocate time for our exploratory activities so that we stick with them. If you want to become a serious explorer dedicated to your growth journey, you need to set aside nonnegotiable time for learning. If you have a long commute to work, listening to a book or a podcast would be more efficient than allocating extra time in the morning to read a physical book. Instead of spending excessive time on social media or texting, read a book.

Swap a reality TV show that you learn nothing from for a documentary. Make learning a social activity on weekends by joining a book club or taking a course. If you're willing and resourceful, you'll find countless ways to carve out educational time in your day.

- **Allocate time to review learning goals.** As you complete your learning goals, take stock of your progress and how far you've come. This will motivate you because you'll see how much progress you've made. It also gives you a chance to consider if you would still like to pursue other learning goals on your list in case you've changed your mind. Update this list monthly, quarterly, biannually, or annually, noting your achievements and the areas that need improvement.

With these parameters in mind, you're ready to create your personalized information diet.

Here is an example to help you get started:

Learning goal: *Become a better salesperson so that I can close more deals and get promoted to a sales manager position.*

Type of information I'm looking for: *How to negotiate better, understand customer psychology, make better and more convincing sales pitches, and determine the customer's needs.*

Sources and learning modes: *Articles, books, online courses, mentors, workshops.*

The time that I'll dedicate to this specific learning goal: *Morning time before going to work, lunch break, weekend afternoons.*

Step 5: Make learning a lifestyle

Learning is so much more than an activity that you occasionally dabble in. It's a way of life. A Nomadic Soul knows that the whole objective of being alive is to grow and evolve.

The fictional character Indiana Jones is a great example of someone who made learning a lifestyle. He was constantly in research mode, asking questions during his day job as a university professor. But he quenched his thirst for knowledge while on his adventures. Whether he was excavating decrepit ancient sites filled with snakes, skeletons, and booby traps or escaping Nazi soldiers, he maintained his curiosity and always looked for clues to feed his mind and inform his next steps.

We can all be like Indiana Jones by proactively making learning an essential part of our life. In addition to cultivating a learner's mindset and staying committed to our learning goals and schedule, here are some ways that you can make learning a lifestyle.

1. Learn something new regularly. Novelty is unquestionably one of the best ways to break out of a daily rut. New learning stimulates your mind and creates new neural pathways in your brain. You can explore new turf by simply taking a different route to work or exposing yourself to other music, books, art, and movies. You can avoid your usual weekend haunts and try going somewhere unknown to you. The possibilities are endless, as long as you're willing to get outside of your comfort zone and follow your curiosity.

2. Be part of a dynamic learning community. According to studies, whoever you spend the most time with is who you become. If you want to develop your explorer muscles, it makes sense to choose your company wisely and spend time with people who have a passion for learning and who stimulate your thought process. There's no shortage of events where people gather to learn more about topics that interest them, whether for personal growth or to sharpen their professional skills. The structured format of these events can make learning more effective and offer opportunities for engaging with like-minded people.

3. Get curious about people and their personal stories. Everyone in the world has an interesting story worth sharing. Each can teach us something valuable. Imagine if we could all approach other people with an openness to listen to their stories and know more about their life and personal beliefs. We would have the privilege of accessing different life paths and traversing unique journeys through the stories and lessons they learned thus far. We would also get in touch with our humanity as we find out about the challenges and difficulties that other people face. In turn, this might inspire us to search for ways to contribute to causes that alleviate those problems. For example, when you speak with victims of abuse, you get a close-up of the visceral pain that they experienced, which can spur you on to support other people like them.

4. Find teachers and mentors to guide you. The wisdom that we glean from other people's experiences can be an invaluable source of learning. If we can find mentors or people who have already succeeded in doing what we dream about, seeking their advice can help us make progress. They can teach us strategies and tactics that can help us avoid making common mistakes and get ahead of the game. Seek out wise and learned individuals willing to take you under their wing and give you knowledge and advice that come from experience. If you have any elders you respect in your family, take them out for a meal and ask them what key lessons they've learned in their lifetime. They might have great advice for you. And both of you will benefit from the exchange.

5. Travel. Traveling can be one of the most mentally stimulating experiences to spark your curiosity. Travel expert Rick Steves once said that "travel is rich with learning opportunities, and the ultimate souvenir is a broader perspective." Traveling is one of the most effective ways to bring out the explorer because you step out of your everyday routine. Your mind is more open to new knowledge and input from new places. Even if you can't get away for a long time, try your best to plan a road trip to a nearby destination. Ideally, you want to go to the places that pique your curiosity and allow you to explore new terrain. If you don't have the means to travel to your desired destinations, watch travel shows or attend cultural events in your town while you save up for those dream trips.

Become an Explorer of Life

To see your life as an adventure, you must take on a big-picture perspective. This panoramic view helps you look beyond the limited parameters of our sometimes superficial material existence. When you have a bird's-eye view of your life, you can see it from a symbolic point of view. Develop an empowering story around the themes, characters, and narrative of your life, and let that story motivate you to become the hero of your own journey. You can thrive right where you are now by learning about just one new thing that lights you up. As writer Brené Brown once said, "We're wired to be brave; that's why we never feel more alive than when we're being courageous." So tap into your courage to get out there and explore.

NEED #3

Express Oneself

Each one of us is a unique expression of the universe. There will never be another living organism with our specific configuration of DNA and the myriad characteristics, temperaments, and talents that stem from it. We all have something valuable to say, whether that be expressed through art, science, numbers, imagination, or thoughts.

Case Study: Maya Angelou (1928–2014)

"I believe that the most important single thing, beyond discipline and creativity, is daring to dare."

An early traumatic experience changed Maya Angelou's life forever. Already used to dealing with racial prejudices as an African American living in rural Arkansas, Maya, at the age of eight, suffered something no little girl should ever have to go through: her mother's boyfriend brutally raped her when they were alone together.

Initially, she told no one. He warned her not to. But eventually her older brother coaxed it out of her when he noticed her behavior had changed. They had always been close, having been brought up together by their grandmother following their parents' divorce. Her mother's boyfriend, Mr. Freeman, was apprehended, tried in court, and subsequently jailed for his actions. After serving his jail sentence, Mr. Freeman was killed by Maya's uncles, who kicked him to death.

This was devastating news for Maya, and she blamed herself for his death. Traumatized by the experience, she became frightened by the power of her own voice and vowed not to speak ever again. Later she said, "I thought, my voice killed him; I killed that man, because I told his name. And then I thought I would never speak again, because my voice would kill anyone."

You might think someone as comfortable with self-expression as Maya Angelou would have spoken up straightaway about what happened to her, but she was almost silenced by the traumatic events she experienced.

This incident drastically changed her personality and approach to life. She became socially withdrawn and decided to leave Long Beach, California, where she lived with her mother, to return to her grandmother in Stamps, Arkansas. Maya felt a deep connection with her grandmother and was comforted by her strong presence, having spent a significant part of her formative years with her. While living there, she developed an interest in writing. By the age of nine, she was actively pursuing her writing, with the encouragement and support of her grandmother. However, she remained detached from others, choosing to compose poems detailing her experiences and feelings to connect to her inner voice. She delighted in her own musings, which she later claimed helped maintain her sanity. Self-expression is crucial to our mental health. If Maya hadn't found an outlet for her pain or to express her thoughts on the injustices she saw around her, her life may have turned out very differently.

While Maya honed her skills as a writer, her grandmother introduced her to her friend Bertha Flowers, the wealthiest Black woman in Stamps. Bertha was instrumental in mentoring Maya and bringing her up to believe in herself as a woman and as a writer. She lent Maya books to read, and through her influence, Maya began to develop into a budding poet. Maya was lucky to have two strong female mentors in her life who encouraged her to articulate herself through language. Many people don't have a support network they can draw on. Expressing yourself authentically may require some degree of rebellion against traditional beliefs. Not everyone will appreciate our authentic expression, yet we must still find the courage to share our thoughts when we believe we have something valuable to say.

Maya once said that there's no greater agony than bearing an untold story inside you. Having been silenced by her abuser at a young age, this is a truth that she was aware of on a deep and visceral level. She was fortunate to have discovered vehicles of expression, such as writing and poetry, early in her life and to have loved ones support her in finding and developing her voice.

Once she found her stride, she was unstoppable. Her unique style of prose began to blossom. Her writing exploded with poignant verses about controversial issues, such as rape and racism, which spoke to the hearts of millions. She excavated life's more profound truths through vivid and colorful anecdotes. People loved her because of her authenticity and her ability to convey her message, which she drew from the depths of her soul.

After finishing her schooling in Stamps, Maya relocated to San Francisco to continue her studies. Once she arrived there, she considered the idea of working instead of returning to academia. She lived during an era where the oppression of Black people was a stark reality in society. She believed that obtaining higher qualifications would be of no use as it wouldn't alter the disadvantages she faced as a Black woman. However, she didn't let that feeling or her lack of higher education stop her from pursuing her passion for writing and sharing her thoughts with her audience. She later became a professor of American studies at Wake Forest University in North Carolina and was often referred to as "doctor" despite not having a college education. Challenging conventional thinking helps us break free from the cage in which society and our own fear of failure tries to keep us contained.

Maya entered the workforce with her eyes wide open, determined to find ways to earn a living by expressing her talents and gifts. Maya tried just about everything, from jobs such as a fry cook to Calypso singing and dancing. Unfettered by the trauma from her childhood experiences, she was willing to do whatever it took to make it in life and pursue her passion as a writer.

Maya's writing time was sacred, and she created strict conditions to protect it. Setting these boundaries gave her time to think and produce her best work. She liked to write in near-empty hotels with no art on the walls that could distract her. "I try to keep home pretty," she said, "and I can't work in pretty surroundings. It always throws me." And so each morning she would leave her house at 7:00 a.m. and head to the hotel to check in to a modest room, where she wrote until 2:00 p.m. The only thing she kept with her was a Bible, dictionary, deck of cards, and a bottle of sherry.

Convinced of the power in her words, Maya was always deliberate and thoughtful in her speech. Her eloquence commanded the respect of listeners and left a powerful impression. She modeled the importance of finding one's voice and expressing it to others. Whether we do it on a stage or a page, what matters is that we develop the courage to speak out and share our truth. As she once said, "A bird doesn't sing because it has an answer, it sings because it has a song."

Throughout her life, Maya did not hold back from advocating for tolerance, equality, and justice. She influenced people to move in the direction of beauty, peace, and wisdom. She encouraged us to take pride in our knowledge and not be afraid to stand up for causes that are important to us. Our skills and passion for making a difference need to come from within. We should give ourselves permission to express ourselves and not wait for someone else to grant us this right.

Maya's poetry drew heavily on her personal history, and she used a direct, conversational voice that invited readers to step into her narratives. Her poems and books were an honest and powerful examination of race and gender in the United States and garnered her much respect as a political figure. Maya was active in the civil rights movement, and she became close with civil rights leaders Dr. Martin Luther King Jr. and Malcolm X. She also served as the northern coordinator for the Southern Christian Leadership Conference (SCLC) in 1959.

During those years, she was instrumental in organizing a historic fundraising concert for the SCLC and later served as the director of the SCLC's New York office. There she helped raise funds that allowed Dr. King to challenge Jim Crow brutality, something she experienced and later examined in her books. She used her influence to speak out on behalf of people experiencing racial injustice who may have been too afraid to speak out themselves. In order to make meaningful change in the world, we must use our voices to serve the greater good.

Even after the civil rights movement, Maya thought racism was still "extremely ugly in America," and it's thanks to people like her that we now see people of color in positions of leadership. We owe it to the people who have gone before us to speak up when we see injustice in the world, too, just as they did. Every time we fail to defend ourselves and fight for our rights in the face of unfairness and injustice, we give away our power.

Maya dispensed advice for leading a creative life to women in her 2008 work *Letter to My Daughter*. Through colorful prose and candid anecdotes, she illustrates the importance of sharing our story. Our vulnerability does not weaken us, she insisted. Instead, it makes us stronger. Because of her authentic approach to life, more women were inspired to bare their souls and share their struggles out in the open. Maya once said, "Have the sense to look at yourself and say, 'Well, wait a minute. I'm stronger than I thought I was.' We need to not be in denial about what we've done, what we've come through. It will help us if we all do that."

Maya believed that creativity can be sourced from our stories. In a time when women are more willing to tell their stories and speak their truths, her message feels timely. She encouraged others to share their struggles and vulnerabilities rather than hide them away.

Our stories and experiences are a significant part of who we are. They drive our actions and are the source from which we can retrieve our strongest creative works. Maya's writing offered inspiration and comfort to millions because it came from the depths of her soul. It was raw, daring, and authentic—and it gave the readers permission to get in touch with the disowned parts of themselves so they could express themselves without inhibitions.

Among the honors she received in later life was the invitation to compose poems in honor of the fiftieth anniversary of the United Nations and the life of Nelson Mandela after the South African leader's death. She also composed "On the Pulse of the Morning" in honor of the inauguration of former United States president Bill Clinton. When asked about that experience, she said, "It is fitting that he asks a woman and a Black woman to write a poem about the tenor of the times. It might be symbolic that Black women when looked at are on the bottom of the graph. It is probably fitting that a Black woman try to speak to the alienation, the abandonment, and to the hope of healing those inflictions which have befallen all Americans, that accounts for white Americans feeling so estranged. Somehow a Black woman knows all about that."

On the morning of May 28, 2014, Maya passed away at the age of eighty-six. World leaders, artists, entertainers, actors, musicians, and poets paid their condolences to Maya, including former United States president Barack Obama, whose half-sister was named after her. At a private memorial service, Oprah Winfrey, Michelle Obama, Bill Clinton, and Maya's son, Guy Johnson, gave speeches.

Maya's remarkable life was an exemplary demonstration of the importance of exploring the deeper dimensions of who we are and sharing that with the world. Maya tapped in to every avenue possible to express her voice and talents, from writing books and composing poetry to dancing, acting, singing, and directing.

Maya never wavered from her belief that people belong everywhere and should be free to explore—a personal motto that emerged straight from the vessel of her Nomadic Soul. She encouraged others to do the same when she said, "Try to live your life in a way that you will not regret years of useless virtue and inertia and timidity."

Maya's spirit continues to live on through the legacy she left behind. She modeled the importance of engaging in a life of personal inquiry and developing our own narrative. We all have a story to share and a message that can make the world a better place. We just have to be daring enough to dig deep and say it out loud to our loved ones and the rest of the world. The bits and pieces of the happenings in your life can come together to form a coherent storyline that can serve others.

Instead of letting the ups and downs of life silence you, let them amplify your voice. Allow your distinct perspective to reverberate with meaning and purpose. As Maya once said, "If you are always trying to be normal, you will never know how amazing you can be." A bona fide Nomadic Soul, Maya Angelou broke out of the proverbial "birdcage" in which she was initially trapped and flew out into the world, blazing a trail with her unique self-expression.

Understanding Our Need: The Pain of Silence

There Is a Genius in All of Us

You are a unique expression of the universe. A one-of-a-kind genetic configuration, you can produce something original that no one else can conceive of. You can channel it through art, science, numbers, or thoughts. Just like everyone else, including greats like Maya Angelou, you have your own special kind of genius. You might have a knack for telling riveting stories with your words. This same applies to other people: your neighbor is a great runner; your cousin sings beautifully; Serena Williams is an ace in tennis; Oprah Winfrey has the gift of conversation and connecting with an audience. They have their own geniuses, and you have yours.

People expect a genius to be spectacular; however, this isn't always so. Our geniuses can take different shapes and forms. Genius can be calm, like the voice of the psychologist who helps you go through a horrible divorce. Genius can be loud, like the motor racer in his prime. Genius can be expressed in numbers, as Galileo did. Genius can be found in forgiveness, as is the case for religious martyrs. Genius can be giving, as Mother Theresa was. Genius can be a good negotiator, a great father, an understanding son, a selfless person, a fearless child, a vivid understanding of the wild, and a love for the water, flight, and fight. The seed of genius is embedded in all of our Nomadic Souls, and if we don't invest ourselves in allowing it to take root and sprout, we'll get lost chasing another person's genius.

Yet the genius that can be seen in childhood is often overlooked or isn't acknowledged by parental figures and teachers. There are plenty of children who were called dumb or "someone who would not amount to anything" that have gone on to have very successful careers in their chosen fields. An example is Dr. Ben Carson, who explained how he moved from a dumb kid to a very successful medical doctor in his book *Gifted Hands*. His genius was in his hand-eye coordination. That hand-eye coordination proved to be an asset for neurosurgeons like him who need it to operate on small parts of the body.

There is a genius in all of us, and until we unearth it, we limit ourselves to living a life of mediocrity. A life without passion and fire is a life unfulfilled, irrespective of our net worth. That's why we must seek the genius within us. Our quest is to find what makes us different and project our distinct voice from that exceptional part that lives within us.

Our Right to Creative Expression: A Hard-Won Battle

History can provide deep insight or perspective on the present and help us appreciate what we have. Freedom of speech, which allows us to express the genius within us, was a human right that our predecessors had to fight for. It's been coveted since the dawn of civilization. Those who have gone before us sacrificed their lives to attain the basic freedom they knew was their birthright. They fought against injustice and inequality in the face of oppressive governments and dictatorships.

Throughout history, different groups of people have faced opposition when fighting to win their liberty. These restrictions were enforced by prejudiced groups or institutions that considered themselves or their ideologies to be superior to those they sought to oppress. During different eras, marginalized communities faced fierce opposition for stating their religious beliefs, political inclinations, artistic or scientific breakthroughs, and opinions about pertinent issues. The groups most often targeted were women, minorities, and natives who lived in territories being colonized.

Even today, there are countries where freedom of expression is not granted to people because of political power struggles or cultural and religious doctrines. The truth is that any government, group, or community that seeks to drown out the voices of its people is seeking control and domination. They want to prevent new ideas, thoughts, and methodologies from changing the order that's been established and from subverting state power. These institutions are threatened by novelty because it could take away their power or force them to implement changes they are not on board with.

A well-known historical example of the power struggle between the people and the heads of state is the French Revolution, which took place between 1788 and 1799. The French revolutionaries were no longer willing to succumb to oppressive overlords, and they courageously fought for their right to freedom of speech. The upheaval was sparked by the widespread discontent with the French monarchy and the economic policies that led to poverty and hunger for France's citizens. The revolution resulted in the violent deaths of tens of thousands of French citizens and the execution of King Louis XVI and his wife, Marie Antoinette. In 1789, France's National Constituent Assembly adopted *The Declaration of the Rights of Man and of the Citizen*. The document proclaimed that all human beings are born free and equal in rights, that sovereignty resides in the nation, and that the law is the expression of the general will. The French Revolution is one of the many historical conflicts that are emblematic of the collective Nomadic Soul's freedom to be seen, heard, and understood.

As long as there's fear, greed, and a drive to dominate, the battle to express ourselves freely and openly will continue. On a positive note, we are steadily making progress toward establishing universal freedom of expression thanks to institutions like the United Nations (UN), who created a milestone document in 1948 called the Universal Declaration of Human Rights (UDHR). The document states that "everyone is entitled to all the rights and freedoms set forth in this Declaration, without distinction of any kind, such as race, color, sex, language, religion, political, or other opinion, national or social origin, property, birth, or other status."

Younger generations like Gen Z are increasingly realizing the importance of speaking up and sharing their voice. According to a study by OCAD University titled "Decoding Gen Z Identity Construction in Social Networks through the Paradigm of Branding," 73 percent of Gen Z believe they need greater self-expression to live a happy, healthy life. They also believe that the internet has facilitated their expression. The same study shows that 55 percent of Gen Z say that they find the internet a more creative space than anything they experience offline.

All generations living and working in our modern world should not take this privilege for granted. Most of us reap the benefits of freedom of speech, and we owe it to those who have gone before us, those who had to struggle to win it and deal with harsh consequences for their candor. We also owe it to the societies that still suffer from oppression, bigotry, and old regimes that bar them from speaking up and being themselves.

Developments like this prove that we're gradually opening the door for people to reveal their true thoughts, inclinations, and premonitions without the fear of being reprimanded and vilified.

Keep this in mind the next time you restrain yourself from sharing your views on a specific topic or showing your creative work to others. Your ability to convey your opinions on a level playing field is something that should be embraced with gratitude and cherished. Let it galvanize you to speak up and be heard.

What Stops Us from Expressing Ourselves

Freedom of expression is a fundamental right in most democratic nations. It's not merely a constitutional issue. It is a human rights issue. Even though we enjoy the advantages of living in a free world, we still face obstacles when it comes to living the highest expression of ourselves, some of which are internal and some external.

When people hold themselves back from expressing their voice and talents, we all pay a heavy price. We miss out on opportunity—all the inventions and ideas that could have saved humanity remain untapped. The late evangelist and priest Myles Munroe poignantly captured this truth when he said, "The wealthiest place in the world is not the gold mines of South America or the oil fields of Iraq or Iran. They are not the diamond mines of South Africa or the banks of the world. The wealthiest place on the planet is just down the road. It is the cemetery. There lie buried companies that were never started, inventions that were never made, bestselling books that were never written, and masterpieces that were never painted. In the cemetery is buried the greatest treasure of untapped potential."

There are three main challenges to self-expression that we face on a collective and individual level: societal structures, the fear of failure, and a lack of self-confidence.

Societal structures. Education has undoubtedly played a pivotal role in advancing humanity, but it also inadvertently diminished creativity and originality in children. In a 2010 study, Kyung Hee Kim, a creativity researcher at the College of William & Mary, found that creativity has decreased among American children in recent years. After conducting three hundred thousand creativity tests going back to the 1970s, Kim concluded that children have become less imaginative and less able to produce unique and unusual ideas.

We are born with a remarkable potential for creative problem-solving, which has enabled us to conceive of and create a life that is more efficient and convenient. However, this ability has also been diminished due to the structures we have created. While a nation with a low literacy level is in danger of economic strife, a country with a high literacy level is in danger of mediocrity.

In his compelling TED Talk "Do schools kill creativity?" British author and advisor on education in the arts to the government Sir Ken Robinson cautioned the world about this defect in the educational system. "We are educating people out of their creative capacities . . . I believe this passionately, that we don't grow into creativity, we grow out of it. Or rather, we get educated out of it," he argued. According to Robinson, children are born with creative and extraordinary abilities for innovation and aren't afraid of making mistakes. "If you're not prepared to be wrong, you'll never come up with anything original. And by the time they get to be adults, most kids have lost that capacity," he said.

Most school curriculums streamline thinking because the students are taught to study and think for an exam. Hence, their thinking becomes restricted to the rigid confines of academic instruction. Political indoctrination in schools is also becoming increasingly common, where students are influenced to accept and support certain political ideologies without critical analysis or debate. Such modes of teaching stifle independent thinking and creative self-expression. When we enter the workplace, we might face similar situations if we work in an organization bound by strict guidelines, hierarchies, and protocols that don't give employees the freedom to communicate their thoughts and ideas freely.

Today, there are still many countries and communities around the world that don't grant freedom of expression to their people. Minorities and women are stifled by old regimes and antiquated gender roles that restrict them from speaking their minds and obtaining the training and education they need to build a career in which they can showcase their talents and voices.

Fear of failure and rejection. Self-expression is not for the faint of heart. It takes courage to own one's individuality fully and display it for the whole world to see, especially with the internet and social media, where you can receive instant feedback. While you certainly can gain some fans along the way, there's also a chance of attracting critics, haters, and people who don't really care much for what you do. This group may even include people close to you, such as family members and friends. Without encouragement from others, it can be intimidating to stand up and speak out. Authentic self-expression requires a certain degree of rebellion against the existing order and beliefs—and many people find this intimidating. That's why they refrain from expressing themselves out of fear of what people may say.

For example, astronomer Copernicus did not publish work on heliocentrism until the year he died because he wanted to save himself from the outrage of religious leaders who would condemn his views as heresy and an insult to the church. Like Copernicus, we have to acknowledge the reality that there's never going to be any guarantee that what we say or do will be appreciated by others. In her book on creative living, Amanda Palmer wrote, "When you're an artist, nobody ever tells you or hits you with the magic wand of legitimacy. You have to hit your own head with your own handmade wand."

Lack of confidence in our abilities. As social creatures we like to evaluate ourselves based on others' perspectives. For example, in the workplace, some employees will never offer their opinions at staff meetings, regardless of the originality of their ideas, simply because they view themselves as inferior to others. This is especially true if we think we lack the influence and platform to create impact. Without the traditional forms of power, we are incapable of seeing ourselves as significant players in the world arena. Most times, our feelings of inadequacy are a result of not being confident in what we have to offer.

When you do not know yourself enough and haven't reached a state of personal acceptance, there's a tendency to feel inferior to those who have embraced their individuality. However, the disparity you feel between yourself and others is not real. You are as good as anyone. You are the only one disparaging yourself and dimming your light.

Even those who are incarcerated, who the rest of society might see as "lesser," are able to write books and essays while in jail. Nelson Mandela's book *Conversations with Myself* was a collection of his writings, many of which he composed while in prison. During his one night spent in jail for refusing to pay a poll tax that was funding a war with Mexico, Henry David Thoreau wrote his most famous essay, "Civil Disobedience." If a prisoner can unleash their artistry despite being confined to a dark, dingy, and desolate cell, so can you. The only thing that can sabotage your self-expression is you. Being daringly different and bold in a sea of sameness requires courage and a strong belief in your convictions.

The Importance of Expressing Ourselves

As breathing is essential to life, so is self-expression critical to the vitality of our Nomadic Souls. Expression is a natural proclivity that can be traced to as early as infancy. From an early age, despite their limited verbal and psychomotor abilities, children often seek ways of communicating their needs to their parents and caregivers, whether through a gurgle or a tantrum.

Life itself is an expression of the cosmos. The main difference between the living and the dead (literally and metaphorically) is simply the ability to communicate through our words, body, and creativity. As long as you're alive, you have the power to voice your thoughts, feelings, and opinions. Here are three reasons why expressing ourselves is important:

1. Self-expression is crucial to the crystallization of our identity. It is the portal through which people can express themselves on their own terms, based on their perceptual ability. This, in turn, helps shape their self-concept. That's why one of the best ways to decipher an individual's personality is by analyzing how they express themselves through their words, actions, and choices.

2. Self-expression helps us access new insights and perspectives on well-being and welfare of the public. In most organizations, when there's a paramount issue on the table, there's always a brainstorming session and board meetings where ideas and opinions are generated from community members. The objective is to gather various views on the matter at hand because the more diverse the thoughts, the more creative the solution.

3. Self-expression is critical to our mental health and well-being. Open expression has been found to promote mental wellness, while a lack of it causes ailments and sickness. In her book *The Gifts of Imperfection*, author and researcher Brené Brown said, "Unused creativity is not benign. It metastasizes. It turns into grief, rage, judgment, sorrow, shame." She expands on this in her book, saying, "There's no such thing as creative and non-creative people. There are only people who use their creativity and people who don't. Unused creativity doesn't just disappear. It lives within us until it's expressed, neglected, or suffocated by resentment and fear."

The ideas and concepts we refuse to bring into the open often become a burden. A lack of ability to express ourselves induces a state of restlessness and dissatisfaction. This is precisely why most forms of psychotherapy usually begin with a self-disclosure session. When the issues weighing on the patients' minds find an outlet, they experience relief as they release the pain of holding on to their stories. When we're going through rough times, such as a breakup or a divorce, self-expression helps us overcome the pains and adjust to reality, whether we channel that into art or confide in others about it.

Famed Mexican artist Frida Kahlo began keeping a diary when she was about thirty-six years old. At that point in her life, she was divorced and remarried to her longtime partner, Diego Rivera. She had endured several miscarriages and undergone many surgeries. She had also lost her father a few years earlier. Kahlo's diary was more than an artistic outlet. It was where she could heal through her reflections. The drawings, scratch-outs, and layers of text all relay her pain and loneliness. Whether we choose to express ourselves to process pain or to share our gifts or make our voices heard, our Nomadic Soul calls us to channel that energy, just as Kahlo did.

Our society belongs to no one individual. It belongs to everyone. Since opinions shape society, everyone must cooperate in building and shaping it by expressing their voice and talent. Imagine if Thomas Edison, Eleanor Roosevelt, Martin Luther King, and Muhammad Ali all decided that what they had to say would not have a lasting impact on others. Just think of all the amazing discoveries, inventions, and social changes that we would have missed if luminaries like these withdrew from their Nomadic Soul missions.

Like these individuals, we, too, can benefit humanity if we believe in ourselves and what we have to say. Whether it's your knack for number crunching, compassion for the needy, or nimble dancing moves, you can use your voice and talent to leave a legacy that people will thank you for long after you're gone.

Digging Deep: How to Show Your Genius

How to Meet Our Need to Express Ourselves

If you weren't encouraged to express yourself and hone your talents while growing up, the prospect of unearthing and sharing your talents can be intimidating, no matter if you're sharing yourself on a world stage or with a close inner circle. This is especially true if you believe that you lack influence, talent, or a platform on which to make significant contributions. If you're convinced that you need the traditional forms of power, such as money, status, and position, you may see yourself as an insignificant player whose voice won't make a difference in the grand scheme.

But the truth is that you don't have to be a celebrity, politician, or a CEO to make an impact with your thoughts, ideas, and opinions. You can be an effective influencer within the sphere of your own workplace, family, and community. Even if it's on a smaller scale, you can touch the lives of the people around you. For example, you can tap in to your love for baking to make brownies every Sunday for your neighbors. If you are passionate about saving animals, you can volunteer at a local animal shelter. Love to sing? Share your recording sessions on YouTube. If you are passionate about a particular global issue, share your thoughts on a blog or in an article.

There's no shortage of ways you can channel your passion. The internet has leveled the playing field and given us a global stage on which we can showcase our best—whether it's on a TikTok video or in a blog post. There are publications in virtually every area that exists. Most nations now enjoy the freedom of speech, allowing their people to share their views and have their say through their votes.

Being daringly different and bold in a sea of sameness requires courage and a strong belief in our convictions. It's easier to follow the crowd and let others dictate our path, but we can overcome this tendency by convincing ourselves of the importance of being heard and rising to meet our potential. Here are a few ways by which you can overcome a fear of self-expression and share from a place of authenticity:

Step 1: Believe that you have something valuable to say

Sharing your message with the world begins with you. You need to believe that you have something valuable to share with others. There will never be another living being with your characteristics, temperaments, and talents—your *vision*. Once you understand this and value it, you will begin to unleash all the potential that lies within you. Your genetic heritage requires a legacy only you can actualize through your works and deeds.

If you ever find yourself struggling to find value in your self-expression, repeat these empowering affirmations to get back to center:

> *"I give myself room for expression."*
>
> *"My creative energy is limitless."*
>
> *"My creative voice flows freely."*
>
> *"I'm ready to share my authentic expression."*
>
> *"I attract brilliant ideas."*
>
> *"Today I am making time to create."*
>
> *"Divine inspiration surrounds me."*
>
> *"I choose to express my authenticity."*

Step 2: Identify the root cause of your fear and shift it

Sometimes the fear of expressing ourselves runs deep. While repeating affirmations can help, it is a superficial solution for those of us who have subconscious fears and trauma that block us. You may have a fear of authentically expressing yourself if you often find yourself repeating these statements such as:

"I don't want to sound preachy and be a know-it-all."

"I'm too boring and unimaginative to come up with anything original."

"I have nothing valuable to offer others."

"I'm afraid of offending others."

"No one will listen."

Identify your limiting beliefs and make a note of them. There's always an experience behind every limiting thought pattern. It will be worth your time to reflect on which specific life event resulted in your fear-based belief system and to begin thinking of ways to transform it. You can do this on your own or with the help of a qualified therapist. Be patient during this process, as it does take time to shift old paradigms.

When it comes to changing your subconscious belief systems, there are several effective modalities that you can look into, such as cognitive-behavioral techniques, neuro-linguistic programming (NLP), tapping, and much more. In addition to these tools, here are three more things you can do to manage any deep-seated fears that get in the way:

- **Don't fight the fear.** Resisting and ignoring the fear will only make it stronger. You need to look the tiger in the eye and tackle the issue head on. You'll notice that fear quickly dissipates if you simply feel the fear when it shows up. You can move through fear with greater ease by triggering the body's natural calm response via closing your eyes and taking deep breaths. Focus on the areas where you feel tightness and tension in your body and slowly breathe into it.

- **Create a support system.** Much like Dorothy in *The Wizard of Oz*, we need people around us who can support us with words, advice, and comfort during our journey. For this reason, we must build a network of friends, family, advisors, and mentors who can be our champions. These people cheer you on every time you succeed and step in to give you a hand when you stumble on the road to authentic self-expression.

- **Keep challenging your fears.** If we challenge our fears by doing the things that get us out of our comfort zone and require us to be braver, we'll gradually build our courage. If you have a fear of heights, try skydiving. Scared of creepy crawlies? Visit an insect zoo. Afraid of public speaking? Join Toastmasters, a nonprofit educational organization that teaches public speaking skills. By consistently pushing your limits, you'll send the message to your subconscious mind that you have what it takes to deal with any potential obstacles you might encounter whenever you attempt to speak your truth.

Step 3: Figure out what you want to say and how you're going to say it

Now that you have the tools and know-how for keeping your fears about self-expression in check, the next step is to figure out what you want to share with the world. Each of us is a product of life experiences, lessons, and challenges that others can learn from. Based on our story, we can share advice with others who might be seeking the insight and knowledge we can offer.

Make a list of the knowledge and experience you would like to bring into the world. Refer to your responses to the exercises on developing authentic identities. Your core values, interests, hobbies, skills, and areas of expertise might offer clues about what kind of content you can put out there.

Once you know what you want to share, find a platform from which you can broadcast your message. In a crowded media space, where so many people are sharing their thoughts on blogs, YouTube videos, and social media profiles, you may feel that your message will be drowned out by all the other voices. You may look at social media stars with millions of followers and subscribers and believe you could never measure up to that. But this sort of fear-based thinking will only sabotage your success. Remember that they all started on the ground and had to work their way up to get to where they are now. And with dedication and focus—so can you!

Let altruism guide you on your mission to express yourself, not your ego. Your message needs a clear and ethical channel from which to come forth. If you are the chosen messenger for a certain cause, you must listen to your heart and catch that spark of inspiration urging you to take action. Using your story to help others gives it meaning and purpose. You'll elevate yourself to another level when you use it to serve others.

Sharing your message does not have to be a grand production. It can be done quictly and discreetly, behind the scenes and away from the spotlight if that's what you prefer—like a prop master that creates movie sets for blockbuster films or an aeronautic engineer who builds spaceships that jet into space or an artist who sells their paintings to support a good cause.

You also want to make sure that you're expressing yourself in a way that is well received by others. They should be able to relate to and understand what you're saying. Key in on the solutions and takeaways that will benefit others. Don't make it all about you. You can share your story, but, in the end, offer a nugget or two of truth that can enhance others' lives.

Depending on the reach and the impact that you would like to have on others, you can select one or more of these five ways to share your message with the world:

- **Write about it.** If you believe that your message comes across best in writing, you'll find plenty of opportunities to share your message through the written word. You could start a blog or write articles and share them online or in print publications. You could write journals or contribute to the company's newsletter within your professional sphere. If you want to reach a larger audience, you could write a book, an e-book, or a column for a newspaper or magazine.

- **Speak about it.** If you prefer to speak your message, you can look for speaking opportunities available within various groups, organizations, and speaking bureaus. These institutions are always looking for speakers who can educate, train, and enlighten their members. Nowadays, you don't have to speak in front of a live audiencc. You can do it behind a computer screen on online platforms like podcasts, webinars, social media, or YouTube videos. You can share your thoughts in meetings, networking events, and informal events such as parties and gatherings if you find people who you think could be potentially interested in listening to you.

- **Campaign for it.** A campaign is an active and intensive way of sharing your message. It will require more of your time and energy. If you're passionate about your cause and want to influence more people, running a campaign is the best way to do it. Campaigns usually run for a fixed period and have an organized set of activities scheduled. It could be as rigorous as the political campaigns run by politicians or as low-key as the small campaigns run by students in school or college. Campaign efforts will require you to recruit a team of people who share your vision and can help you carry out your mission.

- **Teach about it.** You don't have to be a schoolteacher or a parent to be a teacher. All of us can impart knowledge to those who need it most. As a parent, you can teach your children; as an aunt or uncle, you can teach your nieces and nephews; and as a friend, you can impart knowledge to a friend who needs your support. If you're specialized in a specific topic or skill, you can teach in formal settings such as a workshop, seminar, class, or online educational platform.

- **Use your art.** If you're creatively inclined, your art form can be a potent medium for expressing your beliefs. Whether through painting, sculpture, music, dance, or acting, you can use these as vehicles to spread your messages and connect with the hearts of those who resonate with your work. For example, legendary singer Michael Jackson used his music to spread messages of love, equality, and compassion through songs like "Heal the World," "Man in the Mirror," "Black or White," and many other hits. Actor Sidney Poitier only chose roles aligned with his beliefs and showcased issues important to his community, such as *Lilies of the Field*, *To Sir, with Love*, and *Guess Who's Coming to Dinner?*

No matter your age, race, economic, or social status, know that you have a message that could improve the life of someone out there. If you feel the urge to speak your truth, grab that mic and unapologetically share it with the world. Your demonstration of courage is what you need to evolve your Nomadic Soul.

Step 4: Be authentic in your self-expression in all areas of your life

Self-expression is not limited to what we broadcast to the outside world. It also includes how we communicate in our immediate surroundings. As a Nomadic Soul, your aim is to be as authentic as possible in your interactions with everyone around you: family members, coworkers, significant others, and acquaintances. In doing so, people will not only get to know the real you but grow to respect you for the courage you demonstrate in speaking your truth, no matter what.

Here are four guidelines on how to make authentic self-expression a standard in your life:

- **Speak up for yourself.** Every time we fail to defend ourselves and fight for our rights in the face of unfairness and injustice, we give away our power. An indicator of high self-worth is not allowing anyone to say disrespectful or mean things to us that aren't constructive. We must protect ourselves by building healthy boundaries or even putting these people out of our lives if we have to. Being authentic in self-expression means overcoming the urge to please, perfect, pretend, or prove yourself. You'll be brave enough to confront others about the things that bother you and stand up for what you think is right.

- **Speak up for others in need.** If you witness any acts of cruelty or injustice around you, stand up for what you believe is right and speak up for the victims. If we remain silent, we allow the bullies and offenders to get away with harmful behavior. For instance, if someone picks on an innocent coworker in the office, be willing to support them. If someone is not given the right to do something in a public setting because of discrimination based on their appearance or status, speak your mind—but only do it if you're doing it from a place of love and integrity. In this way, you use your voice to fight the good fight and serve the greater good.

- **Express your individuality in the physical.** We can express ourselves not only through our words and actions but also in other areas of life, such as our style, our home decorations, the vehicles we drive, our career and social media feed, how we manage our finances, and even how we choose to parent. Every aspect of our life is an expression of our thought process. Instead of giving in to fads and societal expectations, we should express our authenticity in all outward manifestations of our individuality and create our own rules.

- **Grant others the freedom of expression.** Allowing others to share their ideas freely is just as important as giving ourselves the freedom to do so. This entails keeping our judgments about others in check, especially when we encounter people who are different from us or who hold different beliefs or values than we do. While we should stand by our personal beliefs and ethics, we can learn a lot if we remain open to seeing the truth in what others think. This is especially important in the age of social media, when platforms abound with opinions, thoughts, and creative works.

Instead of following the footsteps of haters and critics who fixate on the faults of others, allow yourself to be fascinated by how the distinctive configuration of a person's personality traits, family background, culture, schooling, and life experiences shape their perspective. When we clear our minds and hearts, we open the doorway for greater understanding and empathy in our interactions.

Creativity: The Highest Form of Self-Expression

Every one of us is born with tremendous creative potential. We possess traits and special talents, which can only be channeled through the right portals. It's up to us to make our creative potential come to life with our rich and fertile imaginations.

Creative living is like a treasure hunt, an adventure to unearth the jewels that the universe has planted deep within us. The search for these jewels can transform a mundane existence into a magical one. Once we find the courage to push past those barriers, we'll have access to the grace and transcendence at the heart of a creatively driven existence.

Freedom of creative expression is everyone's birthright because we are all, ultimately, creatives at heart. As Nomadic Souls, we are at our happiest when we can discover, learn, and create by listening to the whispers of inspiration within us. When we support and advance our own originality, we can leave our indelible footprint in the sands of time and the hearts of those who benefit from it.

PART 2

Connection

NEED #4

Connection with Our Inner World

As Nomadic Souls, we are on a quest to discover ourselves, internalizing what we witness through experimenting, learning, and reflecting as we go along. We want to find our true selves—the version of us that we know we're destined to become. To find real freedom, we need to enter the gates of our interior world.

Case Study: Sidney Poitier (1927–2022)

"I learned to hear silence. That's the kind of life I lived: simple. I learned to see things in people around me, in my mom, dad, brothers, and sisters."

When Sidney Poitier accepted the 2001 Honorary Academy Award, he said that when he had arrived in Hollywood at the age of twenty-two, it was different from what it is today. He recalled that when he came to Hollywood in 1949, "The odds against my standing here tonight fifty-three years later would not have fallen in my favor. Back then, no route had been established for where I was hoping to go, no pathway left in evidence for me to trace, no custom for me to follow. Yet here I am this evening at the end of a journey that in 1949 would have been considered almost impossible."

How Sidney came to defy the odds against him was thanks not only to his extraordinary acting talent but also to his ability to have successfully cultivated an inner world that sustained him during the trials and tribulations he faced during his long career in Hollywood. He credits his self-awareness to his parents and his childhood experiences on Cat Island in the Bahamas. In his early years on Cat Island, he spent much quiet time alone in nature. This time was instrumental in helping him cultivate the rich interiority he remained deeply entrenched in for the rest of his life. It also taught him how to understand the many layers of his personality.

His upbringing gave him the wisdom to know when to fight and when to play it cool—an indicator of a well-developed inner world—because he knew that as a Black man living in America during that era he had to walk a fine line between diplomacy and assertiveness.

In a 2000 interview on *The Oprah Winfrey Show*, Sidney shared his philosophy on our different personas. He said that we all have different selves including a public self, a private self, and a core self. Collectively, these different aspects of our personality help us put our best foot forward. But the private self is fundamental to who we are, housing our fears and frailties. "It's like a clearinghouse where our demons are safe," he said.

The core self represents our pure instinct, where our goodness and capacity for kindness emerge. "When people say, 'I feel it in my stomach,' that's the core self. Our best comes from there;

we know how courageous and honorable we are. The core self is who we are," Sidney explained.

Sidney grew up in an environment without radio, television, or other mediums that could have distracted him from focusing on what really matters. There he could enjoy the simple things, nurture deep relationships, and find meaning and purpose in his life. In his memoir *The Measure of a Man*, he wrote, "In the kind of place where I grew up, what's coming at you is the sound of the sea and the smell of the wind and momma's voice and the voice of your dad and the craziness of your brothers and sisters . . . and that's it."

In this quiet space, he built a solid sense of self, rooted in self-worth, that gave him the resilience and determination to see his efforts through while maintaining his dignity. During his early upbringing, he developed his moral compass, which gave him a sense of right and wrong from early on. It wasn't until he moved to Nassau at the age of ten that young Sidney saw his first automobile and had his first experiences with electricity, plumbing, and motion pictures. In today's modern world, where we have endless distractions, many of us struggle to connect with our thoughts and emotions. We operate on autopilot. We prefer to believe narratives that support our existing sense of self rather than lean into the discomfort of challenging this image of who we are and what we know.

By the time he arrived in Miami at age fifteen to live with his brother's large extended family, Sidney described himself as an immigrant kid with an "inner eye," a "Cat Island curriculum" that gave him the ability to navigate the risks and opportunities he would later encounter. Throughout his journey, which was riddled with detours and setbacks, he remained introspective and deeply connected to the values that he grew up with. In every choice he made in his personal and public life, it was important for him to honor his parents' legacy and align with the principles he was raised with. Being aware of how our personal history and experiences—good and bad—have shaped how we see the world allows us to reflect on which values we want to perpetuate and which we want to change.

After living with his brother for a year, Sidney moved to New York City. He was sixteen years old, and living in the big city was tough for a boy as young and inexperienced as Sidney. But he was determined to make it on his own. He managed to find work as a dishwasher and went through several jobs in this capacity. He developed an interest in acting but failed his first audition with the American Negro Theatre because he could barely read his lines due to his lack of a formal education.

Instead of taking the easy route and quitting, he learned to read with the help of an elderly Jewish waiter and refined his acting skills. Once he realized that his Bahamian accent could also hinder him, he decided to get rid of that too. For the next six months, he got to work practicing and training with the goal of achieving theatrical success. Sidney was unperturbed by challenges because he saw them as an inevitable part of his personal evolution. He admitted that "we are imperfect creatures," and we should try "reaching for the better you, the better me." Like Sidney, instead of fixating on the pain and difficulties, we can use them to rise above obstacles. "We have to reach out, not just to each other, but to the universe," he said.

Satisfied with the progress he had made, he auditioned for the American Negro Theatre again. This time he got in, but he didn't get off to a good start. The audiences didn't accept him, and critics dubbed him "tone-deaf" and said he had an "inability to sing." Most Black actors at the time were expected to know how to sing. This, however, did not discourage Sidney. He had found the world he wanted to be a part of, and he was determined to do whatever it took to master the skills to advance his career. His efforts to improve paid off, and he was noticed, winning a role in the Broadway production *Lysistrata*. Although the show only ran for four days, Sidney received an opportunity to understudy for a role in the movie *Anna Lucasta*. He accepted the invitation, and by late 1949, Sidney was already choosing between an assortment of lead roles on the stage and an offer to work for Darryl F. Zanuck in the motion picture *No Way Out*. Deciding that the film offered greater exposure and learning prospects, Sidney chose to work for Darryl F. Zanuck, and the film debuted in 1950.

In the film, he plays a Black doctor treating a Caucasian bigot, and his performance drew acclaim from audiences and critics. He was offered more parts, each role more prominent than the last—especially when compared to the roles most African American actors were being offered at the time. Finally, in 1955, Sidney got his first breakout role in the film *Blackboard Jungle*.

In 1958, he became the first Black male actor to get nominated for an Academy Award for his role in the film *The Defiant Ones*. While he didn't win on that occasion, Sidney became the first Black man to win an Academy Award for Best Actor for his role in the 1963 film *Lilies of the Field*. Although satisfied with the honor, Sidney had overriding concerns that the award was more of a self-congratulatory one by the industry "for having him as a token." He worried he would be typecast, limited to roles in which he plays the soft-spoken appeaser.

Despite his success, Sidney was criticized for being typecast as an over-idealized African American character who wasn't allowed to have any flaws. His character in *Guess Who's Coming to Dinner?* is an example of this. Sidney acknowledged the criticisms and admitted that he was aware of the pattern, but he was deeply conflicted. On the one hand, there weren't many roles for Black actors. On the other hand, he felt obliged to set an example with his characters by challenging negative stereotypes since he was the only Black actor being cast in leading roles in the American film industry at the time.

Sidney's inward-looking disposition, coupled with his ability to ground himself, informed his performances and role choices. He was committed to the idea that what one does for a living is a reflection of who one is. Instead of seeking "confirmation bias" from others for the roles he chose, he carefully chose to play dynamic and assertive characters with something uplifting and positive to convey about humanity. As a result, Sidney was instrumental in portraying a bold new image of an African American man during the turbulent era of the civil rights movement, when his people were subject to unjust racial stereotypes. He proved that it is possible to stand shoulder to shoulder with his white counterparts and have a powerful impact on culture and society.

In his memoir *The Measure of a Man*, he wrote about how important it was for him that his work should be a representation of his personal values. He felt fortunate to have acted in movies like *Lilies of the Field, A Patch of Blue, Guess Who's Coming to Dinner?*, and *To Sir, with Love*, which he said represented the "collective consciousness" of Americans of a particular era but are still relevant today.

Sidney's achievements weren't limited to the film industry. He recorded an album with composer Fred Katz called *Poitier Meets Plato*, where he recites excerpts from Ancient Greek philosopher Plato's works. On the album, he recites numerous passages from various Plato writings focused on justice, truth, the higher self, and the nature of the human soul. Sidney also became involved in diplomatic work. He served as an ambassador of the Bahamas to Japan from 1997 to 2007. He also acted concurrently as the Bahamian ambassador to UNESCO.

Sidney described himself as a searcher—a person who was always fueled by constant questioning. Throughout his rise from poverty to fame, from an illiterate dishwasher to a wise, legendary actor, he stayed humble, never allowing his status to go to his head. He explained that he was accustomed to solitude and enjoying his own company since his early days as a young boy living on Cat Island, where he wandered alone. This ability to disconnect from the ensuing "mad pace of life" once his acting career began gaining momentum shielded him from external influences, such as the "shock of racism." In his book *Life Beyond Measure: Letters to My Great-Granddaughter*, he wrote, "No matter how much of a public life I went on to have, I never shed that first skin . . . I was not a social person at all when I decided to become an actor."

Life Beyond Measure, which he wrote in his seventies, is filled with the wisdom he absorbed throughout his journey. It made sense of what he perceived as a long and complicated life with many twists and turns. Writing the book did not indicate that he'd found all the answers to life's questions; instead, it was an exploration and exercise in self-reflection.

"I felt called to write about certain values, such as integrity and commitment, faith and forgiveness, about the virtues of simplicity, the difference between 'amusing ourselves to death' and finding meaningful pleasures—even joy," he said. Sidney understood that being self-aware doesn't make us egotistical and self-absorbed. Instead, it holds us accountable for our actions and allows us to live an authentic life aligned with our beliefs, goals, and vision.

Undoubtedly one of the most successful actors in the history of Hollywood, Sidney enjoyed an illustrious career that spanned several decades. He will be remembered not only as a pioneer who shattered the racial glass ceiling in Hollywood, paving the way for the Black entertainers who followed him in later years, but as someone with one of the most prolific bodies of work in film history. The power and influence he channeled through the characters he played on screen are expressions of his Nomadic Soul, which was born from years of deep, deliberate introspection.

Sidney Poitier exemplifies someone who unabashedly took pride in having a rich, nuanced, and varied inner world, which he cultivated and maintained with utmost care. This inner world helped him add depth to the characters he played, which led to his superior artistry. But it also made him a man of high morals and integrity—an exceptional role model for anyone who wants to embody the true essence of a Nomadic Soul.

Understanding Our Need: First, Know Thyself

Entering the Depths of Our Interior World

As Nomadic Souls, we have a lot to gain when we delve into our inner sanctum—we do this through experimenting, learning, and reflecting. True freedom can be found when we take the time to develop our interior world. In his novel *Invisible Man*, Ralph Ellison captures the liberation we experience in reflection, writing: "When I discover who I am, I'll be free."

Reconnecting with our interior world gives us access to the most exalted version of ourselves that we know we're destined to become. Investing the time in understanding ourselves better will make us aware of both our gifts and our shortcomings. Psychologists and philosophers have observed that this longing to know ourselves better has existed since the early years of humanity. The first signs of it can be traced back to fourth century BC, when the priestesses of ancient Greece inscribed "know thyself" on the frontispiece of the Temple of Delphi.

Self-awareness is the conscious knowledge of one's character and feelings. In his book *Emotional Intelligence*, Daniel Goleman suggests that self-awareness is "knowing one's internal states, preference, resources, and intuitions. It is a key cornerstone to emotional intelligence." When we're cognizant of our thoughts and feelings, we can pursue things that make us better, happier, and healthier—the things that honor our Nomadic Soul.

In 1972, psychologists Shelley Duval and Robert Wicklund developed the self-awareness theory. They proposed that "when we focus on ourselves, we evaluate and compare our current behavior to our internal standards and values. We become self-conscious as objective evaluators of ourselves." In this way, we monitor our growth and develop personal standards, which we refer to when evaluating our decisions and behaviors.

However, awareness of our inclinations should go beyond just accumulating knowledge. This journey into ourselves involves more than just reading self-help books and doing personality tests. It's about understanding what's occurring within us, both good and bad, from a place of openness, compassion, and curiosity. Even at our worst, we can acknowledge our blind spots—zooming in on those limiting beliefs and compulsive thought patterns that influence our decisions and actions. We also need to know our personal history and how past conditioning and experiences have shaped us and the way we see the world.

The world is a neutral place. We are the ones who give it meaning based on our perceptions and interpretations of what happens around us. Our understanding of life depends on how our inner world processes the world around us. William Shakespeare highlighted this truth through his character Hamlet, who says, "There is nothing either good or bad, but thinking makes it so." Being rooted in your inner world will endow you with the ability to perceive circumstances in ways that are self-affirming, empowering, and constructive.

Why Most People Lack Self-Awareness Today

If knowing oneself is so critical to our well-being and future, why aren't more people self-aware? Why are we so disconnected from our thoughts and emotions? The answer is that we are simply "not there" to observe ourselves. In other words, we're not present enough to pay attention to what's happening inside or around us. Our focus is often squandered on distractions outside ourselves.

People in the modern world are busier and more distracted than ever. They scurry from one task to the next without carving out enough time for reflection and contemplation. With all this attention on everything else but themselves, very few take the time to pause and tune in. They miss the opportunity to check in with their thoughts, emotions, and body, which are constantly in motion. Psychologists Matthew Killingsworth and Daniel T. Gilbert found that half of the time we operate on "automatic pilot" or are unconscious of what we are doing or how we feel, as our mind wanders somewhere other than here and now.

In addition to the constant mind-wandering, there are cognitive biases impacting our ability to accurately understand ourselves and how we feel. We prefer to believe narratives that support our preexisting sense of self. For example, if we believe that we are reliable and loyal friends, we are likely to interpret events to align with that image. Even if we do something that does not align with these traits, like missing a lunch date with a friend, we don't let it tarnish our image of ourselves. This skewed perception is due to cognitive dissonance, which is the discomfort a person feels when their behavior does not align with their values or beliefs.

For her book *Insight*, organizational psychologist Tasha Eurich conducted a series of surveys where she found that 95 percent of people consider themselves to be self-aware, while only 10–15 percent actually possess this quality. Besides feeling disconnected and unaware of how we behave and why we behave the way we do, Eurich says that we are inclined to see ourselves in a positive light. This delusion is due to the "cult of self," a trend that, with the rise of social media, has caused us to become self-absorbed. We lack the ability and willingness to see ourselves for who we are, making improvements where necessary. This grandiosity of self has caused us to move further away from the Nomadic Soul essence of humility and empathy.

Additionally, confirmation bias can trick us into searching for or interpreting information that confirms our preconceived notions and beliefs. Have you ever felt that when you've accepted a job offer, you are still looking for extra assurance that it is the perfect job? That is confirmation bias at its finest. Even if the signs tell us otherwise, we focus on evidence that we have made the right choice so that we feel good about our decision. If we're going to cultivate our self-awareness, how do we reconcile that with all these psychological loopholes that cause us to acknowledge certain versions of ourselves while resisting humility and self-honesty?

In his TED talk, Daniel Kahneman explains the difference between the "experiencing self" and the "remembering self" and how this affects our decision-making. He argues that how we feel about the experience in the moment and how we remember the experience can be very different, and that they share only a 50 percent correlation. This difference can significantly impact the story we tell ourselves, the way we relate to ourselves and others, and the decisions we make, even though we may not notice the difference most of the time. We need to evaluate our narratives from a non-biased perspective and with a greater awareness of our blind spots.

Some individuals equate being self-aware with being egotistical and self-absorbed. After all, if someone is constantly thinking about themselves, how can that person make room to think about the well-being of others? People with this misconception fail to understand the distinction between an arrogant individual, driven by fear and insecurities, and a self-aware person, driven by curiosity and self-love. If someone is full of themselves, they lack compassion for others. But when someone is in touch with their inner world, they want to share their abundance with others. The Nomadic Soul wants to know themselves intimately so they can serve others in bigger and better ways.

The Heavy Price of Being Disconnected from Ourselves

Research shows that being detached from our internal selves can harm our health in numerous ways. It can cause depression, anxiety, physical ailments, and health complications from living an unhealthy lifestyle. It's in this turbulent state of being that the presence of our Nomadic Souls is diminished, and we're left to our egoic devices.

When we feel disconnected from our insights and feelings, we live in a vacuum, cut off from everything that makes life beautiful. Instead of filling our cup with love and connection, we try to fill the void with superficial things that don't fulfill us. We develop a sense of lack and become needy for attention and love, pushing people away when we feel we don't get those things. The idea that we're unworthy and incomplete becomes a self-fulfilling prophecy as people distance themselves from us because of our clinginess and need for others to complete us.

This inner void can metastasize in the mind, causing mental health conditions like depression. It's been repeatedly proven that self-abandonment is one of the major causes of disconnection from self. Like a child who feels lost without the warm presence of a parent, our inner child feels helpless when we ignore our feelings and fail to process them with loving care.

When we fail to process our pain, we lose touch with our humanity. Not only do we indulge in self-destructive behavior, but we also display hostility, rage, and violence toward those around us when we become disconnected from ourselves. The disconnect that we experience blocks our ability to feel love and compassion toward other beings and treat them with kindness. As Martin Luther King Jr. said, "Darkness cannot drive out darkness; only light can do that. Hate cannot drive out hate; only love can do that."

But facing darkness scares us. Our first instinct is to suppress the darkest side of ourselves and conform to societal norms. The parts of ourselves that we don't reveal lie behind a veil of decorum and niceness. This unsavory aspect of our persona manifests as the shadow self. The shadow self is a part of us that houses everything we have difficulty accepting: rage, negativity, deceit, greed, and any other primitive impulses. Pushed into the deep corners of our subconscious mind, the shadow self is forgotten until it rears its ugly head.

The disowned shadow self reveals itself in addiction, self-sabotage, low self-esteem, anger, and sometimes violence and abuse. It's not uncommon to see seemingly normal people do something outrageous. How often have we heard people who knew murderers say, "But they seemed so normal!" Your shadow self craves to be seen and understood. Shining a light into the shadow will help us reach a whole, integrated self. We begin to love and accept ourselves because we've seen, acknowledged, and worked on our good, bad, and ugly.

Our creativity and passion are also negatively impacted when we're disconnected from ourselves. When we are shut off from our inner world, we block the intuitive guidance and creative insights that add vibrancy to our life and that give us the wherewithal to thrive in our professional and creative pursuits. We lose that zest for life we once had as kids, and life becomes boring and pointless.

Ultimately, people who lack self-awareness miss out on the gifts that lie buried in the deeper layers of their being. These gifts give meaning and purpose to our life. Without the valuable perspective that comes from reflection and contemplation, everything in life becomes mundane and sterile. Like a satellite that falls out of its orbit, we drift away into a dark space of nothingness.

Benefits of High Self-Awareness

Committing to building a relationship with ourselves means investing time in the things we enjoy doing. This protects us from being lured away from ourselves by the capitalistic, materialistic, and reward-based doctrine of the world. When we are tapped into our inner world, we already have our own roadmap for joy and personal success. This map comes from knowing who we are and what we're capable of doing and then applying that knowledge in our everyday life.

Greater self-awareness will also benefit those around you. When your mind is clear and your heart is open, you are more empathetic and aware of others' feelings and opinions.

High self-awareness also improves decision-making and leadership abilities. In this state, your mind isn't clouded by biases and the societal pressure to fit into a particular mold. You can understand the dynamics that run the world because you know who you are, and you have taken responsibility for your life and the direction you want to take it.

The Nomadic Soul's journey of self-awareness is a cathartic process in which we unlearn all the dysfunctional habits we have become accustomed to. We have more freedom to confront our darkness and its enablers. This is an essential piece of self-awareness: embracing our wounds and prioritizing the healing process. Only when we identify and accept our areas of improvement will we start growing into the person that we long to become. Only by attaining self-knowledge can we courageously venture into dark corners of our psyche that prevent us from having a positive impact, both within and around us.

Creating an environment where we hold ourselves accountable for our actions eliminates enablers from negatively influencing us and leading us in the wrong direction. Embracing ourselves allows us to bring the very best out of ourselves, guiding us toward a path where we can experience the most freedom and happiness. A limited existence will give us a constant nagging discomfort deep within that won't go away, no matter how much we try to deny or numb it. Authentic living begins only when we get that proverbial monkey off our back. Taking the time to reflect is the perfect way to live from the center of your Nomadic Soul.

Here are twelve more benefits of having a high degree of self-awareness:

1. A purposeful and meaningful existence.
2. A feeling of balance and being rooted.
3. High emotional intelligence that gives us the ability to understand our feelings, thoughts, and behavior and manage them in a healthy way.
4. Understanding the actions of others and responding in a thoughtful (versus a reactive) way.
5. The ability to identify your strengths and areas of improvement.
6. Living an authentic life aligned with your beliefs, goals, and vision.
7. The ability to stay resilient and composed in the face of change and challenge.
8. Insight to see the higher purpose and significance of each life experience.

9. More fulfilling relationships with people who are trustworthy, caring, and positive.
10. The ability to build boundaries and say "no" when needed.
11. Openness and curiosity to new experiences and information.
12. A willingness to use our talents and strengths to improve the conditions in the world.

Digging Deep: How to Make Your Self Your Sanctuary

How to Meet Our Need to Connect with Our Inner World

Nowadays, we're inundated with information and data. Our culture has become outward-looking. People are now hooked on the latest news, trends, fads, and any opportunity to boost power and status. It's no wonder that, as a society, we're feeling increasingly disconnected from our real selves.

We're also consumed with different priorities and responsibilities that are all vying for our attention. If we give in to these, we feel cut off from our feelings, become desensitized, and lose touch with our thoughts and emotions. Our existence becomes a monotonous routine of dry practicalities, which we believe serves us in our race to the top. A person living this kind of existence feels perpetually drained and unfulfilled. They don't realize that they're losing themselves to the whims and fancies of the people and institutions that control them with constant stimulation in the forms of social media, advertising, sensationalized headlines, and political propaganda.

The good news is that there are ways to handle the stimulation and distractions that tug at our coattails. We can pull back and change our focus by simply shifting our attention inward. When we do this, we add texture and harmony to our experiences by cultivating a rich interior world. In an instant our life changes from grayscale to Technicolor.

You don't have to live the glamorous life of a celebrity or an ascetic one of a yogi to create a vibrant interior world. Anyone can develop a bountiful inner life, but it does require a commitment to spend time alone with our thoughts and feelings. Scheduling some quality "me time" to self-reflect and connect with our unique selves is essential to developing a rich inner life. Another benefit of having an inward focus is that you become a person of substance, depth, and character, especially if you prioritize your personal growth.

Four Steps to Creating a Vibrant Inner World

The following four steps will guide you through this exciting process of building and nurturing a vibrant inner world, an essential aspect of our Nomadic Souls.

Step 1: Commit to a regular practice of self-reflection

If we're busy running around between places, jumping from one activity to the next, it's almost impossible to tune in. We must slow down and carve out time to be in our thoughts and feelings. During these mini-retreats, engaging in daily rituals will give us the mental clarity our mind needs to wander without any pressure and noise.

Here are seven practices that you can add to your daily routine to stay connected with yourself:

- **Meditation.** Meditation is a mindfulness practice where an individual uses a technique such as mindfulness or focusing their mind on a particular object, thought, or activity. Meditation isn't about becoming a different person, a new person, or even a better person. It's about training your awareness and getting a healthy sense of perspective. You're not trying to turn off your thoughts or feelings. You're learning to observe them without judgment. And eventually, you may start to better understand them as well. To experience the benefits of meditation, regular practice is necessary. Choose from the various meditation tracks, videos, and scripts available to customize your meditation sessions. It takes only a few minutes every day. Once ingrained into the daily routine, meditation becomes the best part of your day.

- **Journaling.** Maintaining a journal involves the practice of keeping a diary or journal that explores thoughts and feelings surrounding the events of your life. There are several different ways to do this. Journaling, like all stress management and self-exploration tools, works best when done consistently, but even occasional, sporadic journaling can be stress-relieving when the practice is focused on emotional processing. Another effective form of writing is automatic writing. This is a way to tap into your inner wisdom and deepen your connection to yourself. Grab a notebook or journal and start by asking yourself questions such as, "What do I need to know today?" Listen for the answer and write it down. The trick is not to overthink your writing but to let your pen flow across the page without editing, judgment, or guilt. This is especially helpful when we feel stuck. We often already have all the answers we need. We just need to uncover them.

- **Walks in nature.** Walking meditation is an excellent way to explore your inner world. Whether walking through rugged mountains or traversing through a dense forest, you can tune in to your inner self and return to your most authentic self, devoid of all the external influences you usually face. It allows you to appreciate the pure essence of your being and deepen your relationship with yourself.

- **Visualization.** Visualization is a potent tool to enhance self-awareness and focus the mind on defined outcomes. You can stimulate a powerful attraction to what you want by simply holding an image and viewing it in detail for as little as half a minute! However, it's important that while doing this, you shut down the mental chatter and the fearful voice of your inner critic, which can fill you with doubt and indecision. Take time out during your day to meditate on your vision while gradually building the detail. Use this time to center yourself and relax, let go of expectations, listen to your inner wisdom, and surrender. Make a conscious effort not to get attached to your vision and to take on the role of an objective observer. During this time, it will serve you greatly to take note of any relevant dreams, streams of consciousness, messages, signs, or omens you might experience. These are clues about what's happening in the deeper levels of your being.

- **Present-moment awareness.** Being mindful of the present moment is an effective way to anchor yourself in your Nomadic Soul. Cultivating a habit of focusing on what is—not what might be or what was—is a happier way to live. Relationships can end, status shifts, and beliefs can change, but now is a constant. Awareness is just an exercise in focus. You can get more done while removing fears and stresses from life by redirecting your attention toward what you're currently doing, feeling, or experiencing. Instead of floating into the imaginary landscapes of the past and the future, we ground ourselves in present times and improve our relationship with them.

- **Bodywork and physical activities.** Bodywork is an umbrella term that encompasses dozens of fields of study, modalities, and concepts related to massage, touch therapy, and spa services. Considered an alternative medicine, bodywork can mean anything related to treatment or self-help that focuses on physical healing, movement, or general wellness. Not all bodywork forms involve touch. Some treatments might use water instead of physical contact or address the body-mind connection using the body's energy field. In choosing a modality, listen to what your body needs and flow with it rather than forcing yourself to do something that feels cumbersome. Go for a run in the park, dance around your kitchen, attend a workout class, or hit your yoga mat. Choose to do what feels expansive and freeing to your body. Really feel what it is like to move and stretch your body, noticing any sensations that come up for you.

- **Feed your mind.** Just as your body needs a healthy diet, your mind needs a nourishing information diet. Feeding your mind with new ideas and information is essential to evolving as an individual. Every morning, dedicate at least fifteen to thirty minutes to reading material that enlightens and enhances your knowledge. Don't read just to be entertained; read to stay informed and broaden your horizons. Try to consume more content that is actionable and directly relates to your goals and aspirations. As the saying goes, "information is power," and the more informed you are, the better choices you'll make in your life.

Step 2: Engage in the creative arts and express your creativity

Our inner world is the bedrock of our creative instincts. There are jewels buried deep within us, which shine with the sparkle of creative potential. When we engage in introspective activities that allow us to capitalize on enriching experiences, we'll unearth those jewels within us. Have you ever heard a piece of music or watched a movie scene that gave you goosebumps? That's because there was something in the work that profoundly resonated with you. Watching movies, reading literature, listening to music, and attending concerts, sporting events, or stage shows can invigorate your senses and give you a richer grasp on subtle human emotions and nuanced perspectives. It can be the spark of inspiration needed to awaken a part of you that you haven't discovered.

In addition to witnessing different art forms, our creative impulses can be sparked when we channel our own voice. Spiritual teacher Wayne Dyer once said, "When you squeeze an orange, you get orange juice because that's what's inside. When you are squeezed, what comes out is what is inside." This is especially true in the contributions we make because they reflect our character and what we value the most in life. All of humankind's most prominent artists and luminaries had a vibrant inner landscape that they tended to carefully like a garden. Just think of the inner world of someone like Vincent van Gogh, Jane Austen, or Wolfgang Mozart. All the significant contributions they made to our society and global culture—the artwork, novels, and musical compositions—resulted from all the skills, ideas, and principles they tirelessly cultivated within themselves during their life. When we share our creative gifts with others, we're essentially giving them a glimpse into what we're all about in a poignant and discernable way.

Step 3: Adopt the student mindset

We have the choice to believe that life is happening *to us* or *for us*. It's up to us to choose to actively participate or to sit on the sidelines. Adopting a student mindset will remove us from a passive stance where we assume that everything occurring is random and haphazard. When we embody this mindset, we view all life events as serving a purpose, assisting our growth and evolution into better people.

When we become a student, life becomes a school. Upon facing challenges, we should ask ourselves questions like, "What is this here to teach me? How can I improve based on what I am learning? What purpose is this serving in the long run?" In engaging in this inquiry, we're compelled to go within in search of those answers.

Other people's stories are a rich source of learning and an effective way to bring awareness to our own traits and narratives. Storytelling has been a major source of entertainment since the dawn of humanity. Whether it's tales of Hercules from ancient Greek mythology or the quests of fictional heroes like Luke Skywalker in *Star Wars*, stories have the power to activate the emotional center of our brain and inspire action. We can paint a picture in our mind's eye and experience things vicariously. Indulging in a good story, whether through a novel, movie, or even an interesting anecdote that a friend shares with you, will light up your neural networks and transport you to different worlds.

Step 4: Monitor the quality of your thoughts

Our brains work like marvelous pieces of machinery when we know how to shape and nourish them. If we want to use them effectively, we need to understand their basic structure and how they contribute to shaping how we think and feel about ourselves and the world. As you learn more about how your mind operates, you'll develop a newfound respect for its role in your life, and you'll be more inclined to take better care of it.

Ever since you were a kid, you have crafted stories and stored them in the deep recesses of your mind. You may not be aware of it, but many of the decisions you make today are based on these old, unexamined beliefs lodged in the deep recesses of your subconscious mind. For this reason, it will be well worth your time to do a "mental excavation" to dig up any limiting ways of thinking that need to be replaced with more empowering ones.

To become more aware of your thoughts, you have to take on the role of the gatekeeper of your mind. This role entrusts you with the responsibility of monitoring and scanning your ideas to discern which ones deserve your energy and focus and which do not. Stay in touch with your inner dialogue and how you engage with the world by doing regular check-ins with yourself. Start by asking yourself a simple question: *How do I feel right now?* Note your response. Tune in to your body and notice what it's telling you. Pay attention to that fluttering in your chest or belly.

When times get tough, we often push on and cover up how we feel in an attempt to hold things together. Sometimes we numb ourselves with substances like drugs, smoking, and alcohol or activities like overworking. In doing so, we disconnect from our inner world. We ignore our feelings and emotions that are there to tell us something. Let yourself feel all the senses by starting your own practice of going within. Have the courage to sit with difficult or uncomfortable emotions and fears.

Buddhist nun Pema Chodron says that in pain and crisis there lies a hidden doorway to freedom that appears to us only when we're sure that there is no way out. She encourages us to ask questions like, "What is causing my pain?" and, "What will happen if I simply lean in, keep company with it, hold it with tenderness?" If we're willing to look deeper, we'll find that there is a full sense of aliveness in those challenging times. Be compassionate with yourself and tune in to your breath to keep yourself centered as you look at the wisdom.

The Inner Self: The Seat of the Nomadic Soul

Our inner self is the seat of our Nomadic Soul and our portal to a Higher Force. When we stay connected to ourselves, we can tap into the abundant support available from this benevolent energy. Our self-awareness keeps us rooted in this sanctuary of support and stability. We become immersed in our magnificence and all that we can offer to the world. We learn to honor the need to journey inward and trust the voice of life as it whispers to each of us. When we realize our value and worth, we are able to share our gifts, voice, and talents with others.

NEED #5

Connection with Other Living Beings

No one is an island. Even though we need to occasionally step away to engage in our solo pursuits, we still need a place that we can come home to—whether that be a physical location or people. Having roots makes us feel as though we are part of a community and that we're not alone on our quest. Connecting with others is a fundamental need we must fulfill in order to thrive.

Case Study: Jane Goodall (1934–)

"I like some animals more than some people, some people more than some animals."

It all began with a stuffed chimpanzee.

While other little children were gifted teddy bears for their birthday, Jane Morris-Goodall's father gave her a stuffed chimpanzee named Jubilee. When she reflected back on her treasured childhood companion, primatologist and anthropologist Goodall remembered, "My mother's friends were horrified by this toy, thinking it would frighten me and give me nightmares." Instead, it sparked her early love for animals. To this day, the chimpanzee sits on Jane's dresser in London.

Jane's early research studying chimpanzees influenced our understanding of our species and reminds the modern science community that we are part of nature, not separate from it. Jane showed that chimps have complex social structures just as we do and form loving, caring attachments to their offspring and peers. From her decades of learning and observing chimpanzees in their natural habitat to her more recent years spent educating and building awareness about conservation and solidarity, she's been guided by a deep spiritual and moral conviction to reveal the common thread that connects us all.

Born in London, England, in 1934, Jane's unquestionable love of animals and the African continent have been constant forces in everything she does. Her love influenced her to move to the Kenyan highlands to live on a friend's farm in 1957. While in Kenya, a call from top archaeologist and paleontologist Dr. Louis Leakey to discuss the animals in the habitat landed her a job as his secretary. At the time, Louis Leakey was studying great apes because he believed it could help map the behavioral patterns of early hominids—a taxonomic family of primates that include humans and their ancestors, as well as some of the great apes. Jane accepted the offer and was sent to Olduvai Gorge in Tanganyika (now known as Tanzania), where he laid out plans for her to work.

Louis encouraged her studies, sending Jane to London to study primate behavior alongside Osman Hill and primate anatomy alongside John Napier. Later, he sent Jane to the Gombe Stream National Park along with Hill and Napier, making them the first of a group to visit the park. They would later be known as "The Trimates." Pleased with her work, Louis again secured funds for

Jane to go to Cambridge University in 1962, where she earned a PhD in ethology.

Jane began her journey studying great apes because she believed it could help her team learn more about the characteristics of early hominids. But by the end, she realized she had learned much more. She found a portal into the hearts of these magnificent creatures that illuminated the interconnection between animals and human beings.

Jane's work, beginning with her study of the Kasakela chimpanzee community at the Gombe Stream National Park, shows how well she was able to connect with animals. Jane was only twenty-six years old when she started trekking through the forests of Tanzania to study wild animals. Initially the chimpanzees would run away from her, but after several months of steady interaction, she gradually became a member of their communities—a distinction that had not been achieved by a researcher before.

She gained entry into chimpanzee society by taking a mindful approach toward them. Jane's methods did not go along with conventional scientific approaches for studying primates. Instead, her connection with these creatures was based on instinct, empathy, and behavioral knowledge. In her early days at Gombe, Jane would work alone or with native guides. She spent long hours observing and tracking the chimpanzees in the dense forests, gradually moving closer and closer to them until she could sit with them. With patience and courage, she gained the trust of the animals and made incredible discoveries about their habitat and behavior. This went against the universally accepted practices among researchers, which often prevented them from having any emotional attachment to the animal that was the object of their study. Her fellow academics didn't support the idea of giving chimpanzees names or ascribing emotions to them.

To prove them wrong, Jane took inspiration from an animal that she was already very connected to—her dog, Rusty. "You can't share your life in a meaningful way with a dog, a cat, a rabbit, and so on, and not know the professors were wrong," she said at the 2109 Young World Summit. "And now animal intelligence in particular is something that people are really interested in."

Since the day Jane began her legendary research on chimpanzees in Gombe, she took an unconventional approach to studying her subjects. She did not allow the preexisting ideas about the animals she worked with to influence her. Instead, she observed with an open mind and heart, seeking to connect with the creatures and become their peer. She immersed herself in their habitats, unfettered by her academic knowledge. She tapped into her natural instincts to gain the chimpanzees' trust and develop a personal connection with them. Forging this bond made it possible for her to live with them and interact with them over many years.

One strategy Jane utilized to draw closer to her chimp subjects involved giving them distinctive names such as "Fifi" and "David Greybeard" when she observed them displaying unique behaviors and individual personalities. Jane noted, "It isn't only human beings who have personality, who are capable of rational thought [and] emotions like joy and sorrow." She also noted the display of "human" actions among chimps, such as hugging, kissing, patting on the back, and tickling. This observation made her remark that the gestures were evidence of "the close, supportive, affectionate bonds that develop between family members and other individuals within a community and can persist throughout a lifespan of more than fifty years." Humans are wired for social relationships from which we get comfort, support, fun, and companionship, and it appears chimpanzees are wired the same way.

Through her work at the Gombe reserve, Jane challenged two long-standing scientific beliefs at the time: (1) that only humans had the conscious ability to construct and use tools, and (2) that chimpanzees were vegetarian.

She observed the chimps fishing for termites using long stalks of grass and modifying twigs by removing the leaves to make them more effective. In response to Jane's revolutionary findings, Louis Leakey wrote, "We must now redefine tool, redefine man, or accept chimpanzees as human!"

One day, she witnessed a group of chimpanzees kill and eat a colobus monkey. Jane noted that the chimpanzees at the Gombe reserve killed and ate as much as one-third of the colobus population at the reserve every year. This behavioral observation of the chimpanzees challenged previous conceptions about their behavior and diet.

Jane also noticed that the chimps had a strong tendency of being aggressive and violent toward each other. The dominant females deliberately killed the infants of other females to maintain dominance—sometimes going as far as cannibalism. Jane witnessed Passion and Pom, a mother and daughter, steal and kill babies in their own community. In her book *Reason for Hope*, Jane said of this observation: "During the first ten years of the study I had believed . . . that the Gombe chimpanzees were, for the most part, rather nicer than human beings . . . Then suddenly we found that chimpanzees could be brutal—that they, like us, had a darker side to their nature." There's no denying that her findings were revolutionary and represented a paradigm shift as far as contemporary knowledge of chimpanzee behavior was concerned. It was more evidence of the similarities in social relations between chimpanzees and humans—even though it was much darker. Although humans crave connection, we are not always perfect, sometimes choosing to lash out and hurt each other instead of setting boundaries to protect ourselves and each other.

Watching these creatures engage in almost human-like behavior, such as fighting, consoling each other, and playing, opened Jane's heart and mind even more to the natural world. Her experiences at the Gombe reserve invigorated her efforts to spread her message about the conservation of the planet and become an advocate for animal rights. Her message is ultimately about getting in touch with the humane part of us that yearns to connect with those around us and aspires to embody qualities such as compassion and kindness.

According to Jane, we're all capable of connecting with the world around us if we make time to connect physically with nature on a regular basis. We need to get outside, see green plants and trees, and breathe fresh air. She supports the idea that children should interact with the outdoors and other living creatures. This advice is critical today, when kids tend to be glued to their electronic devices and build superficial connections on social media.

In 1977, Jane founded the Jane Goodall Institute (JGI), which helps support the ongoing Gombe research and efforts to study chimpanzees and their habitats. JGI also has a global youth program called Roots & Shoots. Initiated in 1991, this program helps younger people begin paving their conservation journey, helping them choose topics to study that interest them like pollution, deforestation, and the future of wild animals. Jane says Roots & Shoots does not just teach respect for animals, who we now know are sentient and feel fear and pain just as we do. The program also helps its participants develop respect for our fellow humans of different cultures and religions. By developing empathy, we can cooperate with each other to save the environment, which we are still destroying. "We still have this window of time, and we must get together to make use of that," Jane said.

In the mid-1980s, Jane experienced another seminal moment. As one of the world's leading experts on chimpanzees, she was granted access to several medical research laboratories in the US. There, the chimps, who are almost genetically identical to humans, were held captive and used for medical research. During research, they were often subjected to painful and sometimes fatal experiments.

Jane talked about an emotional encounter she had with one of the chimpanzees during her visit during a speech at the sixty-fifth Beatty Lecture. "I'll never forget the first chimpanzee I saw in one of those five-by-five cages. He was an adult male. I was down on my elbow, and he was looking out at me. Bare floor. People in white coats sticking needles in him. His name was Jojo," she recalled.

"As I looked at him, tears began to roll down my cheek. He reached out with a finger and gently wiped them away. That's when I knew I had to do something," she said. "And it's been a long journey."

Jane continues to be a passionate proponent of chimpanzee welfare to this day. She devotes the bulk of her time to advocating on behalf of chimpanzees and the environment—traveling approximately three hundred days a year to spread her message.

While we may not all be able to devote our whole lives to connecting with and protecting animals and the environment as Jane has done, we must strive to find pockets of time to connect to the natural world around us. It adds dimension to our outlook and reminds us to be grateful for the incredible planet we inhabit.

A slight shift in our behavior and choices, like choosing to stop eating meat or using sustainable products, can create a ripple effect that benefits the whole ecosystem. Jane reminds her audiences and followers to take responsibility for the decisions, big and small, that they make daily. This includes what we wear, how we travel, and what we eat, because everything we do can have enormous consequences for the fate of our planet and every creature who lives on it. We may not be able to stay conscious of every choice we make, but we can contribute to the planet's well-being in our own unique way based on our capacity.

When we unite as a community to solve a local problem, we bring conscious awareness to the kind of policies we have and their impact on our community and the world. In this way, our efforts will all add up to create a cumulative effect, with thousands or even millions of people making more conscious choices that will result in significant shifts. Jane reminds us that "every individual matters. Every individual has a role to play. Every individual makes a difference."

Jane believes that even though humans have been gifted with large, complex, and advanced brains capable of solving and understanding all kinds of problems, we don't utilize them enough for the greater good. There is a disconnect between our heads and our hearts. We yearn for material gain and convenience and don't pay enough attention to engaging in daily acts of kindness or developing a value system that supports the planet.

Despite her concerns, Jane reveals in her *MasterClass* series that she is optimistic and maintains hope for a better tomorrow. Her stories reveal the strength of the human spirit and our ability as a species to overcome challenges. She says that these stories of courage bring us together and reveal the similarities we share with other beings. In the case of chimpanzees, she mentions that there are hardly any genetic differences between us and them. We all feel pain, fear, happiness, and anger, and we share the quest for love. This universal language of emotions connects us to one another and is the gateway we can use to understand and appreciate every entity on our planet.

Jane reminds us that we are connected—humans, animals, rivers, forests, the entire planet. We are all vital parts of a beautiful whole. "An ecosystem is made up of complex interrelationships between plants and animals. I see it as a beautiful tapestry of life. Every time our actions cause a species of plants or animals to become extinct, it's as though we pull a thread from that tapestry. If enough threads are pulled, the tapestry will hang in tatters, and the ecosystem will collapse," Jane said at a panel titled "Reconnection with Nature."

During her long, illustrious career, Jane has looked into the eyes of all types of creatures—dogs, birds, and other primates—and has seen them for the unique souls that they are. She saw that animals had their own needs, desires, and personalities. When we're willing to connect with other creatures, we'll develop the same kind of empathy for one another. We'll see that humans and animals suffer when the planet is harmed. One small contribution, like planting a tree or adopting a pet, creates a positive ripple effect that impacts the entire ecosystem.

Like a true Nomadic Soul, Jane Goodall knows that it's only when our head and heart work in harmony that we can deeply understand all living creatures, including our fellow humans. This is the gateway to reaching our full potential as a species and a planet.

Understanding Our Need: No One Is an Island

Humans Are Wired for Social Relationships

No person is an island. As far back as when an ancient person discovered huddling together helped fight off the harsh cold, human beings have always sought and yearned for a connection with one another. While we occasionally need to step away to engage in our solo pursuits, we want to know that we have a place to come home to—a safe haven where we can unwind and replenish. Novelist George Moore said, "A man travels the world over in search of what he needs and returns home to find it." Having roots makes us feel as though we're part of a community, that we are not alone on our quest. Connection is a fundamental need that we all have in common.

Whether it's a survival instinct or a biological compulsion, we have always craved connection with other humans and creatures. We're meant to be around other people and forge a meaningful connection with others. Studies show that our bodies and minds work better when we're together. We're less prone to stress, and our happiness increases. Even people who give us a hard time provide growth opportunities. They make us aware of our triggers and challenge us to stay calm and centered while we handle difficult circumstances.

Our brains need continual interaction. Withdrawing from other beings can decrease our social intelligence and negatively impact our health. Research has shown that newly born babies must be embraced to promote healthy psychological development. The lack of loving assurance from physical touch can inhibit an infant's normal development and even result in death.

Even as the world seems to be drifting toward an individualistic model that rewards independent achievements, research has proven that we're happier and more fulfilled when we have congenial, cooperative interactions with other people. For example, in a work environment where social connection is prioritized and the sole objective isn't just getting a paycheck, management and coworkers feel better supported. They are driven toward innovation and collaboration. Employees experience kinship and camaraderie in their team, and it imbues their work with purpose.

Living in the Age of Loneliness

In the early times, living together was a necessity. Our hunter-gatherer ancestors required each clan member to play a specific role that benefited their group. There were the warriors and hunters who protected the clan and searched for food. The nurturers stayed home to take care of domestic duties such as child-rearing, cooking, and tending to the sick. The holy person healed and comforted the group.

How is it that we are accessible to each other at the click of a finger, yet we seem to be more distant than ever before? Before the advent of social media, loneliness was already on the rise as Western culture valued independent success and happiness above all else. We saw it as freedom from the once fundamental principles that held society together, such as familial cohesion, settling down, cultivating a sense of community, or even religion. This shift in our values has caused people to move away from the community-based mindset that we once had.

In a capitalist society, biological explanations dominate our understanding of mental health. However, the social, political, and economic structures in a society significantly contribute to the mental health of people. Certain setups that fostered community and cooperation are more favorable to our well-being than others. The nineteenth-century German philosopher Karl Marx was able to foresee the perils of a society that does not value relationships. He stated that an alien society leads to alienated individuals.

Marx suggested that there are certain human needs that are fixed, like hunger and sexual desire, and there are some that originate from the culture and history of society. For this reason, a state must deal with human nature based on what's currently taking place in a specific historical epoch. Nowadays, most working professionals have their basic needs of food, shelter, and safety met. But this self-sufficiency has led to an emerging trend of isolation and loneliness in our society. John Cacioppo, author of *Loneliness: Human Nature and the Need for Social Connection*, states that scholars estimated that 20 percent of people in the US during the 1980s felt lonely at any given time; now, it's thought to be over 40 percent. According to a study by the Mental Health Foundation, those between eighteen and thirty-four years old are at greater risk for loneliness than older age groups (fifty-five-year-olds and up).

In our capitalistic-driven society, we must consider the repercussions of loneliness and isolation that many people experience as a result of working to pay their bills and survive. If professionals are made to work exceedingly long hours in the name of boosting a company's bottom line, they won't be able to have a healthy work-life balance. The relationships, or the chances of developing them, erode and lead to increased disconnection from their social nature.

The rise of texting and social media is also a significant cause of loneliness. These modes of communication are now used as substitutes for in-person interactions. A 2017 study by Kaspersky Lab showed the impact of social media on people's relationships in the physical world. Almost seventeen thousand people in eighteen countries responded to a survey on their use of social media. A third of the respondents to the survey admitted that they now communicate less with their parents, children, partners/spouses, friends, and colleagues because they can communicate with them via social media.

We've become more dependent on online platforms as a source of social connections because of their ease, convenience, and instant validation. These virtual ties delude us into believing that we're well connected. As a result, most relationships are brief, shallow, and impermanent. But chatting with people and liking their posts on virtual platforms is not the same as going out for coffee or a beer with a friend or a group of friends.

The internet and social media platforms create the illusion that a sense of community could be achieved by shortening miles and removing geographical barriers. This has not been the case. With the rise of social media, we have created virtual selves that live seemingly picture-perfect lives. These images have robbed us of the ability to build organic bonds that humans over millennia have developed through shared experiences. We are stuck in a dismal cycle that traps us in our virtual identities. We cannot share our genuine feelings or emotions with anyone, as it would take away from the image we wish to portray. A 2018 National Center for Biotechnology Information (NCBI) study found that high levels of social media use are connected with an increased risk of symptoms of anxiety and depression.

Another reason we're seeing the emerging trend of loneliness is that we lack initiative in cultivating deep relationships due to busy and hectic lifestyles. We've become accustomed to developing connections with the sole purpose of getting ahead in our lives and leveling up. This transactional mindset makes people ask themselves, "What's in it for me?" when befriending others, and their decisions are based on what can be gained from others. The fickle, fleeting, and noncommittal mindset of most individuals today makes genuine and deep friendships hard to come by.

Taking a utilitarian approach to relationships isn't just cold. It's detrimental to us and everyone in our community. Our psychological well-being suffers greatly when we lack meaningful relationships in our lives. Not only are genuine relationships a source of comfort, support, fun, and companionship, but they also offer opportunities for learning and growth.

Relationships Are Integral to Our Growth

Living in a profit-driven, individualistic society does not change the fact that relationships are the bedrock of human life. We're immersed in them from the moment we step out of our door. We wave at our neighbor walking their dog down the street and have a brief yet pleasant exchange with a barista preparing our morning coffee at our local cafe.

Relationships are the connective tissue of life, linking you to your fellow beings around you. A hug from a family member, a fun night out with friends, holding hands with your beloved, or a brief but enjoyable exchange with your next-door neighbor—each of these connections plays a vital role in the tapestry of your experiences.

Each relationship has varying dimensions, time frames, and intensities. As the saying goes, "People come into your life for a reason, season, or a lifetime." Every relationship serves a purpose in our lives, and we're dependent on each other, not only for our physical needs but also for our emotional and spiritual needs. For instance, our friends serve as a sounding board when we're deciding on something in our lives. Our pastor or priest calms us with verses that give us perspective on life and mortality.

Not only are relationships a source of comfort, support, fun, and companionship, but they offer opportunities for personal growth. Some lessons cannot be learned outside of a relationship. Every interaction will bring out different sides of you and allow you to observe your reactions from various perspectives. If you take the time to analyze and reflect on the relationships that have had the biggest impact on you, you'll find an abundance of wisdom and knowledge about yourself. For example, if you're triggered by feedback from a coworker, you can use that encounter to dig deep and find the source. Were you triggered because you're insecure about your abilities or because you assume that your coworker is trying to minimize your accomplishments (or both)?

We're especially prone to having our buttons pushed in our intimate connections with family members and partners. Addressing these relationships can reveal any unhealed inner-child issues and help you discover your triggers. They are like mirrors placed right in front of us to witness all those wounds and not-so-pleasant parts of ourselves that we've been avoiding. Sometimes, we've disowned or hidden these parts of ourselves, but relationships bring them right out for us to face and deal with.

We are what we see in the world, and that's why our relationships are one of our greatest sources of teachings. When we integrate those lessons into our personal philosophy, we accelerate our growth and evolution. Every person we meet serves a higher purpose of furthering our Nomadic Soul's knowledge on Earth, and we attract only those who are relevant to each chapter in our journey.

But we can only extract wisdom from our relationships if we're willing to be accountable for how we treat others and take responsibility for our actions. A person who's defensive and takes things personally does not have the emotional bandwidth to glean wisdom from their encounters with others. A delicate ego and damaged self-esteem will cause a person to be closed off from learning.

If this sounds like you, start by analyzing your most significant relationships and answer these questions:

- Why are/were you drawn to this relationship?
- What did you learn about yourself from this experience?
- What do you think you can change or do better?
- How do you feel about the person/relationship now?

A Chinese proverb says, "Fate brings people together, no matter how far apart they may be." Out of the nearly eight billion people on this planet, you'll have the privilege of getting to know only a handful in your lifetime. Value every single person who crosses your life path, because fate has brought them into your life for important reasons only you can discover.

The Types of Connections Available to Us

What does it mean to connect to something or someone? Does connection happen when you take a long walk at the beach under the watchful gaze of the stars and you feel the universe flow through you? Or does it occur when you have an in-depth conversation with someone who finally "gets" you? One thing is for sure: humans have a desire to connect.

According to the Oxford dictionary, a connection is the action of linking one thing with another. Some connections seem instantaneous, like the flaring of gas when it meets a match, while some are gradual and drawn out.

Making new connections and investing in them is a form of self-care. We can enjoy them even more if we have different types of relationships with a wide range of people. Being in a relationship doesn't always have to involve emotional attachment, commitment, and/or physical intimacy.

In his book *Loneliness*, Cacioppo describes three dimensions that form the basis of human connectedness.

- The first is *Intimate Connectedness*, which refers to the deeply personal and vulnerable connection we usually seek in a romantic and marital capacity.
- The next is *Relational Connectedness*, which considers the need for close companionship and friendship typically observed among friends and relatives.
- The last is *Collective Connectedness*, which refers to our need to connect to a particular group with similar or shared beliefs and goals.

These three dimensions offer a framework for the types of connections we build in our lives that form the basis of our sense of self. They can even influence how we understand and adapt to our environment.

However, as a culture, we don't typically take a holistic approach to our relationships. We tend to put a lot of emphasis on romantic love and pay less attention to the others. Once we find a partner, they and our children come first, and friendships and other relationships become "nice-to-haves." Unlike formal bonds, friendships lack structure, and maintaining them is based purely on availability and convenience. We can go for months and years without seeing a friend, but we can't go for very long without our children or spouses.

Given our hectic lives, prioritization is essential, but we must do it with the knowledge that we need a mix of all types of connections to feel fulfilled. Part of the problem of focusing on only close connections is that we become limited. We need to expand our definition of connection to encompass more kinds of relationships. There's only one word to describe the feeling of love in English, but in Greek, there are six.

According to the ancient Greeks, there is a buffet of love we can feast on. They had six words that capture the essences of love we experience in different types of relationships:

- Eros—sexual passion
- Philia—deep friendship
- Ludus—playful love
- Agape—love for everyone
- Pragma—long-standing love
- Philautia—love for self

Almost every spiritual tradition postulates that love has the highest frequency in the universe. Sufi poet Rumi said, "Love is not an emotion, it's your very existence." By tapping into various forms of love and opening our hearts, we raise our vibration and the vibration of the collective consciousness.

We don't have to limit our connections to just other humans. We can form bonds with animals as well. Almost all of us have had at least one life-changing interaction with an animal that completely impacts how we view other animals. This connection has seen animal domestication increase over the centuries due to our need to connect with species other than ourselves. In today's world, where people are comparatively more isolated and have fewer interpersonal connections, many find stronger relationships with animals. Having these domesticated pets, such as dogs, cats, birds, and rodents, is a heart-opening, therapeutic experience because of the loyalty, companionship, gratitude, and unconditional love they show us.

Our ability to connect with our species and other creatures points to the spiritual nature of our Nomadic Soul's need to connect. Nurturing that need with positive intentions and a caring attitude could save the world and save us. No matter which perspective you choose, one thing is clear: humans are social animals with a need to develop deep, genuine connections with the outside world.

Quality Beats Quantity

Have you ever considered how many authentic relationships you have in your life? This does not include the random people who follow you on Instagram, Twitter, or Facebook. Nor does it include the acquaintances that you meet at fancy soirées, social gatherings, and networking events.

Authentic relationships are reserved for those few people who you know will be there for you, no matter what. If you're ever in a state of distress, you feel comfortable calling them, even late at night. You can be vulnerable with them because they see and accept you for who you are, warts and all.

These authentic relationships can include partners, friends, family, or coworkers. The type of relationship doesn't matter as much as the quality of the dynamic you share with them does.

Most people today can probably count the number of these special connections that they have on one hand. Given the power struggles and discrimination in our society, the steady erosion of moral and ethical values, and the hectic pace of life, this is hardly surprising.

It's challenging to forge deep, lasting connections when we're caught up in our busy lifestyles. Texting and social media are now used as substitutes for in-person interactions. These virtual ties delude us into believing that we're well connected. As a result, most relationships are brief, shallow, and impermanent.

We often fail to realize that real connections based on love, trust, and caring are vital to the nourishment of our souls. Relationships marked by tenderness, understanding, and unconditional love are not a nicety but a necessity when it comes to our psychological health and well-being.

The search for deep and meaningful connection is often seen as idealistic or even naïve to some. They may scoff at the idea as a romantic notion propagated by movies and novels. They may argue that these ideals fuel fantasies that set up false expectations, leading to disappointment.

But sincere and heartfelt connections can become a reality if we truly focus on finding and building them. If we're willing to examine our behavioral patterns and commit to trying to find, develop, and sustain those quality connections, we can find them in the most unexpected places.

Films with moving narratives, like the Oscar-winning masterpiece *The Shape of Water*—a love story between a lonely, mute janitor named Elisa and an amphibian man—vividly demonstrate this possibility of finding profound connection if we're open to it. Elisa had to see through the façade of the sea creature to witness his beauty. Her compassion and openness gave her the courage to communicate and develop a loving relationship with him. Their surface differences didn't hold them back from picking up on their shared commonality—a desire to give and receive love.

The relationship between Elisa and the sea creature illustrates the richness that authentic relationships can add to the tapestry of our life. Our Nomadic Soul journey becomes much more dynamic when we're willing to engage with others more deeply—when we're willing to laugh, smile, and break bread with those we feel strongly connected to.

It's our birthright to have friendships that go beyond the surface-level pleasantries, where we can have a heart-to-heart dialogue in which both parties are empathetic and honest with each other. We all need to feel understood and respected for who we are and to be ourselves without feeling judged.

Here are four guidelines for cultivating authentic and healthy relationships in your life:

1. **Deal with your own stuff first.** True intimacy can be challenging to develop between two people if one or both the parties have lingering issues they're unwilling to work on. Low self-esteem, guilt, anger, and other negative emotions will contaminate any relationship you want to build. Before seeking authentic connections, you've got to be honest with yourself and acknowledge any wounds that need to be healed.

A solid inner foundation will give you the strength to open up to someone in a healthy way.

2. Be willing to invest. Growing healthy relationships takes work and requires a willingness to invest. Like a delicate seedling, our connections need to be regularly tended to, watered, and given enough sunlight and nutrients so they can grow and flourish. We need to carve out enough time and space in our lives to be fully present with another person and truly invest in a relationship. Intimacy develops when we are available to engage in warm and genuine communication, all while respecting the other's values and views and spending quality time with one another.

3. Begin with the intention to give and not get. Most people enter relationships hoping to get something out of it: emotional satisfaction, financial benefits, career advancement, or knowledge. Although there's nothing wrong with wanting these things, it's important to remain wary of being motivated by purely self-centered intentions. The dynamic of a relationship dramatically shifts when we change our attitudes to embody a spirit of giving instead of taking. We should be willing to ask ourselves, "How can I enhance this other person's life? How can I help them?"

4. Only choose those who are capable of reciprocating. Not everyone is capable of having deep and meaningful relationships. You have to be selective and invest only in those who display qualities conducive to building healthy connections. Selfish and immature individuals lack the compassion needed to take on the role of friend or partner. They don't have the emotional bandwidth to be a whole, fully functioning adult in any kind of partnership. Relationships are a two-way street, and both sides need to pitch in to keep it going. Knowing this can save you from the pain that comes from trying to get close to a person who is emotionally unavailable, unbalanced, or reckless.

High-quality relationships require our attention. The more that we engage them, the stronger and more valuable they become. In the end, you'll realize that all the hard work you put into developing these connections is worth it because of the love and joy you gain from them. As a Nomadic Soul, these high-vibration connections are vital for our growth and mission.

Digging Deep: How to Make Planet Earth Your Home

How to Meet Our Need to Build Connections with Other Living Beings

Part 1: Building Meaningful Connections with Other People

No two relationships are alike, even if you are the common denominator. The dynamic you share with another person will differ depending on how your energies blend. When you try on a shoe, only you will know if it fits. In the same way, only you know what it feels like when you interact with a person and spend time with them.

Relationships of all kinds have structures and rules, some predetermined based on social norms and others defined by the two parties involved.

Awareness of how you and the other person relate to and behave with each other will set expectations and make it easier to be a part of the relationship. It also makes it easier to check in with ourselves and gauge whether or not the relationship is aligned with our values.

The most socially accepted relationship structure is the monogamous, committed, romantic relationship. This kind of relationship is heavily idealized by the media. Whether it's the "happily ever after" fairytale romance or the three-carat-diamond engagement ring, we believe that finding that special someone is the be-all and end-all of all relationships. There's no denying that a happy marital connection can be one of the most fulfilling ones we can have, but it's not the only connection out there.

But too many people spend so much of their time searching for "the one." In the process, they deprive themselves of the emotional satisfaction they can gain from other types of relationships. The reality is that there are plenty of options that might be a better fit for you, and you don't have to be limited by the traditional template of monogamous romantic relationships.

Even if you are in a committed relationship, exploring other avenues of getting your needs met, either by yourself or through meaningful connections with others, is essential.

One person cannot meet all your needs, and you'll need to diversify your "relationship portfolio" so you're not overly dependent on your partner. Doing so will put less pressure on them and allow you to focus on the parts of the relationship you mutually enjoy. For instance, if you're not into sports but your partner is, they can plan a regular get-together with their buddies to watch games. It gives them space to experience the kind of camaraderie that comes from bonding with their friends who do like sports.

Creating a variety of romantic and platonic relationships is the key to getting your needs met. For many, consciously choosing relationships may seem unusual and not something that has even crossed their mind.

If you fall into this category, the best way to get started in diversifying your "relationship portfolio" is by going within and asking yourself what it is you want. Here are some questions to consider:

- What do you want from your relationships? Do you want solid connections that stand the test of time, in-the-moment ones, or a mix of both?
- What kind of activities do you see yourself doing with other people? Would you like to attend cocktail parties with them or go on road trips to exotic locations?
- How much time, energy, and heart are you willing to put into your relationships?
- How big do you want your network to be? Would you like it to be large and expansive, or do you prefer a small, intimate inner circle that you build over time?
- What are your current goals and visions for your life? What kinds of people and relationships would be a good fit for where you are now and where you're going?
- What kinds of people do you want to surround yourself with? What kinds of conversations and experiences do you want to have with them? Is it important that you share common views and goals, or are you open to listening to diverse perspectives?

Based on your responses, you can discern target locations where you can meet potential friends. Make time in your schedule to network and spend time with new connections.

Use these five guidelines to deepen your connections:

1. Connect based on commonalities. We all share the same human experience and are more similar than we think. We have similar hopes, fears, and desires, and it's precisely these commonalities that we can use to bond with others. Bonding with others based on shared experiences will make relationships more real and grounded in familiarity, trust, and kinship. For example, all mothers, no matter where they're from, face similar experiences when caring for their young ones. Entrepreneurs from all corners of the globe can relate to each other when speaking about common obstacles they face when managing their businesses.

Even subtle commonalities can be discovered by asking open-ended questions that will get people to open up. They say that everyone you meet can teach you something new. When we are curious about others and ask the right questions, we can learn many interesting things. You never know when you might get a spark of inspiration or a brilliant insight from someone. When you listen to your Nomadic Soul instincts, you'll be curious about people all over the world, even if you don't know them personally. You'll naturally embrace the commonalities and differences you have with everyone you encounter. You're okay with stepping outside your social and familial comfort zone so that you can befriend individuals from other neighborhoods, cultures, and countries.

2. Embrace differences in others. When meeting new people, take on the role of an explorer. Allow yourself to be fascinated by how the unique configuration of a person's personality traits, family background, culture, schooling, and life experiences shapes their unique perspective. If you face any resistance or fear while doing this, you are likely being triggered by unhealed issues from your past. By gaining awareness about our own "stuff," you become more conscious of how you may be projecting your insecurities and judgments onto others. When you clear your mind and heart, you open the doorway for more understanding and acceptance in your interactions.

3. Become a student of human behavior. You can learn something valuable from every person you meet, whether they are a janitor or a tech firm's CEO. Everyone has a story from which we can learn and grow if we're willing to listen to the wisdom embedded in their words. Glean knowledge from others by focusing on what they're saying (and not saying) to you, and ask questions based on what you want to know about them. Observe and be aware of the meaning and feelings behind what they say. Be willing to go beyond your comfort zone and ask questions about anything that sparks your curiosity.

When we come from a nonjudgmental place, other people can sense that and will be naturally drawn to us. You can build a more diverse network of friends from different backgrounds. If used responsibly and with conscious intent, the internet makes it much easier for us to access all kinds of online groups and communities where we can meet diverse people. Besides observing other people's behavior, read books on human behavior that give a more detailed framework you can use when interacting with others in person. There is a plethora of books out there that touch on practically every aspect of human behavior, offering great insight into understanding the fundamental qualities of an individual and how you can use this knowledge to develop beneficial and loving relationships with others.

4. Develop compassion and concern for others. We're all human beings sharing a common experience on Earth. We need food, shelter, and a sense of belonging. We all experience fear and doubts and face uncertainty. We all crave recognition, happiness, and peace. When you reflect on these commonalities and minimize the differences, it's easier to elicit compassionate responses for others. The key to developing compassion is to make it a daily practice. You can send out vibrations of love throughout your day by simply meditating on it during your routines, when you interact with others, and when you reflect on the current state of the world. Everything you think, say, and do matters and has the power to alter your mindset or how you interact with others. Avoid interrupting, judging, and projecting your own preconceptions onto what others say when they open up to you. You can hear the truth behind words when you can fully listen to what others are saying. When you release your judgments, you'll be less inclined to label everything as right or wrong, good, or bad. Others will feel more comforted in your presence and sense that you really do care about them and what they have to share.

5. Help those in need. If you wish to develop your compassionate side further, step outside your ego-driven paradigm of existence and connect with others through regular acts of kindness. Your contribution could be as simple as tossing a few coins or notes to a homeless person on the street or giving up your bus seat for an elderly lady. The more you express your compassion through various good deeds, the more pronounced that trait will become. When you develop your empathetic side, you'll begin to care about pertinent issues around gender, economic, social, and racial equality; world hunger; and human rights because you value all human beings' lives and are willing to be part of the solution. You'll want to use your gifts to bring about change and progress through your efforts to collaborate, innovate, and create. Your solidarity with your fellow human beings inspires you to act.

Learning How to Balance Autonomy with Relationships

As important as having high-quality connections is, we need to balance our time with others with some alone time. Having sufficient "me time" away from others to work on the things that are important to us is vital. For this, we need to build healthy boundaries to maintain some semblance of autonomy and independence in our life.

Autonomy is often a sensitive topic in relationships. Asking for more space can make us appear distant or reclusive to other people. But there's a fine line between interdependence and codependency. Enjoying your family, friends, and partner's time and attention is fine, but considering that you have a life, interests, responsibilities, and social circles beyond the relational bond you share with one person is essential.

If we fail to acknowledge this need, we risk finding ourselves in a codependent relationship—a relationship where an individual's self-image and state of being is bound to the ones around them. The major signs of a codependent relationship include a lack of boundaries. In these kinds of relationships, emotional manipulation, insecurities, and the low self-esteem of one or both partners stifle any potential growth and create a toxic environment.

Interdependence, on the other hand, differs from codependence because the individual has a healthy, well-established sense of self. This helps them be present in a relationship with another person without losing themselves in it. This type of connection breeds affection and understanding. Everyone in the relationship dynamic feels supported and cared for, as opposed to being controlled and stifled.

This is not limited to romantic relationships. A study has shown that stringent parenting styles harm a child's autonomy and ability to build associations during the teenage years. When children grow up in such environments, they struggle to assert themselves as individuals or even show affection when they grow up. Autonomy is necessary for relationships to thrive because it allows us to gain confidence and develop a solid identity.

The first step toward establishing healthy, autonomous relationships is to know what you enjoy and what is of value to you as an individual. Then you can communicate this to your loved ones. Don't be afraid of offending people by declaring your needs and what's important to you, saying "no" when you want to. Always try to carve out time for the things you enjoy. Standing firm within yourself and your values does not diminish the importance of those you love. It only enhances it.

In our digitally connected age, we can have different kinds of relationships with varying degrees of intimacy. Even though many of us are aware of our need for community, putting yourself out there can still be daunting. Most people find this difficult to do because they feel caught up in their busy routines and get stuck in their ways. They miss the opportunities to connect with others on a deeper level. Having authentic connections with other people and other beings requires a conscious effort on our part to create the space and time for them *and* for ourselves.

If you struggle with intimacy because it makes you feel vulnerable, return to the previous chapter on developing a stronger connection with yourself. The exercises can help you deepen your self-awareness and make you feel more rooted in your own sense of self. Creating healthy relationships with others is almost impossible if you feel blocked by your fears and insecurities. Once you can handle your emotions better, it's just a matter of learning social skills and being more mindful of how you relate to others and how you treat them.

While genuine human connections are fundamental to our Nomadic Soul's vitality, we can benefit from extending ourselves to other life forms. Fortunately, we live on a planet home to millions of plant and animal species. Immersing in this biodiversity allows us to develop connections beyond the human realm. In the next part, we will consider the steps that can be taken to feel closer to the natural world.

Part 2: Building a Meaningful Connection with the Natural World

For thousands of years, 99.9 percent of the human experience was lived in hunter-gatherer communities, which gave early humans the freedom to roam through the lands and have direct contact with the flora and fauna on it. Early humans developed an intimate bond to nature and found divinity in their natural surroundings.

This deep reverence gave rise to animism, which is the belief that everything on the planet has a spirit or a soul. This includes rocks, mountains, rivers, animals, and even plants. They believed it was important to respect the spirit of animals by living in harmony with the land and all the creatures that occupied it.

Fast forward a couple of millennia, and we now find ourselves living in a world filled with high-tech marvels made of plastic, concrete, glass, and steel. But these modern conveniences come at a heavy price. We have to deal with side effects like leading a high-stress lifestyle and being exposed to environmental toxins, loud noises, processed foods, and radiation fields.

Even though we're wanderers at heart, with spirits that yearn to be free in the wide-open world, we confine ourselves to a lifestyle that is mostly indoors, sedentary, socially isolated, and artificial. Not many of us city dwellers have the luxury to get off the modern-day treadmill to appreciate a sunset or a night sky, to walk by an ocean or a river, or to take in the magnificence of a mountain range. The demands of a capitalistic society tie us to our desks, often working for long hours.

Depriving ourselves of nature's bounty goes against our very essence and can cause a major imbalance in our system. When we are no longer connected to the earth, we feel worn down and vulnerable to several stress-related diseases like diabetes, heart problems, asthma, allergies, obesity, and cancer.

The solution is for us to find pockets of time in our schedule during which we can get back to basics and connect with the world around us. That doesn't mean that we go back to living the way Neanderthals did—we can just borrow a page or two from them. We can proactively search for creative ways to escape the concrete jungles that most of us inhabit, transporting ourselves into spaces that are wild, open, and relatively untouched by people.

Forging a connection with Mother Nature and the creatures that dwell in it is healing because it allows you to leave your worries behind and experience a renewed sense of vitality and spiritual exuberance. Fortunately, we're not alone on Earth. As of 2018, 1.3 million species of plants and animals have been identified that share this planet with us. They come in all shapes, colors, and sizes and live in all types of environmental conditions.

Connecting with nature is a heart-opening experience that offers a glimpse into a different paradigm of existence. It adds dimension and meaning to our worldview and awakens our love and gratitude for the incredible planet that we live on.

Here are five ways in which we can build a deeper connection with the natural world:

1. **Spend more time in nature.** When you're mired in modern life, you're subject to all the artificial constructs and rules that are a product of human thinking. You may not realize it, but these collective trends, pressures, and norms significantly impact how you think and behave. In a natural environment, you're not constrained by any of this. Your mind can return to its natural state of pure consciousness that

synchronizes with the rhythm of the universe. Find pockets of time in your schedule during which you can get back to basics. Take a walk in the park during your lunch break or type out your novel while sitting on the beach. Grow your own garden and make time to water and prune it. If you have more free time on your hands, go out on treks or camping trips to the closest natural surroundings. Relish the feeling of cool breeze on your face as you take a bike ride by a lake. Bask in the golden rays during sunset on a beach.

2. Raise a pet and learn about other animals. For most of us, the only animals we're exposed to are those we keep in our homes, such as dogs, cats, birds, or perhaps some rodents and reptiles. Having these domesticated pets in our surroundings is therapeutic because of the loyalty, companionship, gratitude, and unconditional love that they show us. You can get better acquainted with other animals by visiting zoos and animal sanctuaries or finding volunteer opportunities in places like animal shelters and rescue facilities. You can also broaden your horizons by watching documentaries about animals on channels such as National Geographic or the Discovery Channel or reading any material that will educate you about the natural world.

3. Respect all living entities on the planet. All creatures belong to the earth, and it's their right to have a place to live here. Yet our advanced technology and knowledge are infringing on those rights. Polar bears are losing their homes because the ice caps in Arctic regions are rapidly melting due to climate change. Forest animals have no place to live as trees are cleared for human activities such as farming and building real estate. Oceans are becoming polluted with toxic waste that's killing marine life. Poaching and hunting have caused the extinction of numerous species. Deforestation has resulted in the loss of trees and vegetation.

We fail to realize that we all belong to the collective consciousness and any harm done to the environment and the creatures that live in it will, in turn, affect us. Besides the extinction of plants and animals, our actions lead to climate change, desertification, soil erosion, fewer crops, flooding, increased greenhouse gasses in the atmosphere, and various other problems. We need to hold ourselves accountable and reestablish our connection to Earth by educating ourselves and the next generation about engaging in eco-friendly and sustainable practices.

4. Advocate for the preservation of our planet. Because of our growing population, we need to create more living space and produce more supplies to sustain everyone. Population growth has steadily created an imbalance in the ecosystem because we have neglected to keep the effects of our actions in check. The fallout from the policies we've implemented in the name of profit has led to severe damage to the environment in the form of deforestation, pollution, a loss of biodiversity, and dead zones in our oceans. We've all learned about these issues in high school, but as adults, we need to revisit them and decide how we can be part of the solution that will help reduce the impact of these threats. You can join a group, volunteer, or educate people about the specific causes that are important to you in your community.

Environmental activism can range from undertaking a volunteer project planting trees to rescuing animals and combating animal cruelty. Remember that even the smallest act on your part will create a ripple effect that'll impact others.

It's a known fact that planet Earth faces imminent threats of destruction caused by the neglect of our environment. We must conserve and protect our only home, which can only happen if each of us takes responsibility for how we treat the environment. A globally conscious person will have no problem shifting to a sustainable and earth-friendly lifestyle and spreading this awareness to the people around them. They would want to recycle, volunteer in environmental groups, protect animals from extinction, or engage in any activity that will work toward conserving all the bounties of nature for future generations.

5. Take inspiration from the natural world. When you're intimate with nature, you'll have the chance to witness the real essence of life in all its splendor and glory. You'll become less cynical and gain a deeper understanding of life as you observe the realities of the prevailing laws that govern nature, like the seasons, cycles, and food chain. Below all the randomness and chaos of humanity, you'll see that a harmonious universal order exists. You'll stop taking life for granted and value every moment, because nature will remind you of how fragile and fleeting life can be. You'll be humbled when reminded of how small you are in the grand scheme of things, which can motivate you to make the most of life and make more contributions.

Planet Earth: My Home

One of our fundamental emotional needs is to feel like we belong somewhere. Not everyone is born into a nation, community, or family where they fit in. Perhaps your values are more aligned with other people or entities that lie outside your immediate surroundings. Or maybe you just don't want to be boxed into a small world you've outgrown. You may want to broaden your horizons and feel "at home," no matter where you are on the planet. You'll feel differently about your place in the world by being an active member of a global community. When you make the effort to connect with the people and creatures that cross your path, you will feel like a global citizen—a resident of planet Earth with a panoramic outlook of the world and the role you play in it. You can intelligently deal with societal issues once you're able to think critically, take on leadership roles, stay up-to-date on information and news about current events, and be proactive about making progress and being part of change.

Once you're plugged into this "oneness" with your celestial home, it'll be easier to figure out your purpose and use your life to benefit others during your stay here. Take your place as a member of the world community by educating yourself about pressing global issues and becoming part of the solution. Use your voice to express your opinions, connect with allies, and start movements to influence policymakers, governments, and organizations through offline and online platforms (like blogs), peaceful demonstrations, and volunteering. This inclination to make a ripple of change originates from the depths of your Nomadic Soul, prodding you to enhance the lives of your fellow earthlings, so heed its call.

NEED #6

Connection with a Force Greater Than Ourselves

Since the beginning of humankind, we have not been afraid to ask the big questions, such as, "Why are we here?", "How did we get here?", and "Where did all of this come from?" In the face of the unknown, we have looked to a higher existence to explain the greater mysteries of the universe. We have searched for meaning, purpose, and comfort by connecting with this higher force through faith practices and rituals.

Case Study: Carl Sagan (1934–1996)

"Somewhere, something incredible is waiting to be known."

As a little boy growing up in Brooklyn, New York, Carl Sagan looked up at the night sky and wondered what was really out there. He gazed at the glittery spectacle above him and asked himself whether there was a possibility that other worlds in space were teeming with life just like Earth.

This precocious boy would grow up to play a pivotal role in astronomy, making the study of the stars popular and mainstream. Among his many breakthroughs during his lifetime, his most significant contribution was the TV series *Cosmos*. In the documentary series, he breaks down complicated topics in astronomy in a compelling way, drawing in millions of viewers and opening their minds to a world of infinite possibilities.

Inquisitive about the celestial realm from a young age, Carl recalled wanting to learn what stars were: "I went to the librarian and asked for a book about stars . . . And the answer was stunning. It was that the sun was a star but really close. The stars were suns, but so far away they were just little points of light . . . The scale of the universe suddenly opened up to me. It was a kind of religious experience. There was a magnificence to it, a grandeur, a scale which has never left me. Never ever left me." Understanding astronomy gives meaning to our place in the universe, especially when we consider that we're made up of many of the same elements as the stars—further connecting us to the skies.

That seed of curiosity was implanted in Carl's imagination and sprouted into a lifelong fascination with science—space, in particular. He was mesmerized by what he read in science fiction novels, which told stories about space voyagers who traveled to distant planets and galaxies. He relished his visits to science museums with his family and school. These early experiences stimulated his desire to explore places that are far beyond what can be seen by the eye.

Initially, he struggled to make sense of the enormity of space. According to biographer Keay Davidson, Carl faced an "inner war" because of the influence of both his parents, who were, in many ways, "opposites." Carl would later trace his analytical urges to his mother—a woman he said "had been extremely poor as a child in New York City during World War I and the 1920s." As a young woman, Carl's mother "held her own intellectual ambitions, but they were frustrated by social restrictions: her poverty, her status as a woman and a wife, and her Jewish ethnicity." For this reason, Davidson notes, she worshiped her only son, Carl, and hoped he would fulfill her unfulfilled dreams.

However, Carl claimed that his sense of wonder came from his father. Although his father was awed by his son's intellect, he took his ability in stride, seeing it as a normal part of young Carl's growing up. Later on in life, after he had become a writer and scientist, Carl would often draw on his childhood memories when making scientific points. In his book *Shadows of Forgotten Ancestors*, he described his parents' influence on his "later-life" thought process. He wrote, "My parents were not scientists. They knew almost nothing about science. But in introducing me simultaneously to skepticism and wonder, they taught me the two uneasily cohabiting modes of thought central to the scientific method."

Carl recalled one watershed moment in his life when his parents took him to the 1939 New York World's Fair at the age of four. The exhibits at the fair were a turning point in his life and greatly impacted his future ambition. He saw several new inventions, robots, and a time capsule filled with messages for the future. Recalling these exhibits, Carl remembered how "when a flashlight shone on the photocell, you could hear something like the static on our Motorola radio set when the dial was between stations," and "when the tuning fork was struck by the little hammer, a beautiful sine wave undulated across the oscilloscope screen." He wrote, "Plainly, the world held wonders of a kind I had never guessed. How could a tone become a picture and light become a noise?"

These early experiences set the stage for Carl's curiosity to explore the unknown and unravel future possibilities. Carl also witnessed one of the fair's most publicized events: the burial of a time capsule at Flushing Meadows. Watching this time capsule thrilled Carl immensely. It would later inspire him and his colleagues to create similar time capsules that would be sent out to the galaxy's far reaches. These capsules were the Pioneer plaques and the Voyager Golden Records, and with them, he was able to assemble the first physical messages sent into space. These were universal messages that could potentially be understood by any intelligent extraterrestrial life that might find them.

As a teenager, when he learned that he could turn his hobby into a profession, he set his mind on becoming an astronomer. After graduating from high school, he proceeded to advance in the world of academia, where he focused primarily on studying planets and exploring the possibility of life in these celestial worlds. He continued, guided by the gravitational pull he felt toward unknown worlds. He was determined to learn all he could through scientific fact and observation rather than superstitious assumptions, because he firmly believed that science could be a pathway to adventure and a portal to the mysterious.

Carl also focused on cosmology, a branch of astronomy that studies the universe's origin and how it has evolved and extends beyond the foundational scientific elements of astronomy. Cosmology involves the philosophical contemplation of the universe, and it has been investigated by famous astronomers, scientists of all stripes, philosophers of space and time, and metaphysicians. Cosmological theories include both scientific and nonscientific propositions, making it possible to experience both awe and understanding simultaneously.

According to Sagan, not only is science compatible with spirituality, but it can be a profound source of spirituality. And he was not the only one to suggest this. Several astronauts who have seen Earth from space have had a profound spiritual awakening. A number of them have experienced significant cognitive and spiritual shifts invoked by feelings of oneness and unity with a Higher Power. Dr. Edgar Mitchell, who was the sixth person to walk on the moon, documented in his scientific biography how he experienced a moment of transcendence and enlightenment on his way back from the moon.

While looking at Earth and the cosmos from his spacecraft window, he acquired a deep knowing of our interconnectedness and how, when we humans get consumed by greed and ego, we miss the big picture. Upon returning to Earth, Dr. Mitchell tried to make sense of the otherworldly sensation he experienced in space, studying ancient Indian religious scriptures. He found that the description of samadhi, which is when someone's consciousness temporarily dissolves into Brahman (the highest state of consciousness), matched what he felt during his spiritual awakening. He described it as "seeing things in their separateness, but experiencing them viscerally as a unity, as oneness, accompanied by ecstasy."

It was this same sense of interconnectedness with something larger and omnipresent that inspired Carl in his scientific findings. It galvanized his efforts to contribute, uncover knowledge, and offer perspectives that could advance humanity and even improve conditions on Earth. Carl's article "The Planet Venus," published in *Science* in 1961, was central to the discovery of Venus's high surface temperatures. It was his view that Venus was very dry and hot instead of the balmy paradise others had imagined or claimed it to be. He proposed a greenhouse model for Venus's atmosphere. His stance on climate change was that it was a growing danger created by humans. He equated Earth's experience of climate change to Venus's natural development into a hot, hostile planet through a runaway greenhouse effect.

Carl was also famous for his research and opinions on the possibilities of extraterrestrial life and UFO sightings. He advocated for skeptical scientific inquiry and the scientific method, pioneering exobiology, a scientific field that studies the origins, early evolution, distribution, and future of life in the universe. He also promoted the search for extraterrestrial intelligence (SETI), becoming the most cited SETI and planetary scientist.

Over the span of his career, Carl published over six hundred scientific papers and articles and authored and coauthored more than twenty books on subjects related to extraterrestrial life. In addition, he wrote a number of popular science books such as *The Dragons of Eden*, *Broca's Brain*, and *Pale Blue Dot*. He was featured as the narrator and cowriter of the award-winning 1980 TV series *Cosmos: A Personal Voyage*. It is the most widely watched series in the history of American public television and has been seen by at least five hundred million people in sixty different countries.

In 1994, he wrote the sequel to *Cosmos*, called *Pale Blue Dot: A Vision of the Human Future in Space*, which inspired the famous image that depicts Earth as a tiny speck in outer space. He used this image to emphasize his views on humanity's place in the universe and the vision we should have for the future. "It has been said that astronomy is a humbling and character-building experience," he said. "There is perhaps no better demonstration of the folly of human conceits than this distant image of our tiny world. To me, it underscores our responsibility to deal more kindly with one another, and to preserve and cherish the pale blue dot, the only home we've ever known."

As an astrophysicist, he felt compelled to communicate the facts, but as a Nomadic Soul, he was drawn to doing this work in a way that was poignant and poetic. Unlike other professionals in the field of science, whose interpretations of dry facts and theories were rather insipid and dull, Carl was a master at weaving together science and evocative storytelling, writing books that inspired millions to open their minds to the cosmos. He did this without using flowery jargon and complex myths that might confuse his readers. Even though his narratives of the stars reflected on science-based realities without any trace of New Age insinuations, he was immensely successful in invoking curiosity and kindling a sense of awe.

Michelle Thaller, assistant director of science communication at NASA, was one of the members of his audience who was inspired by his work. She credited him for being the catalyst in her growing interest in the field when she was a young girl. In an interview where she discussed his impact on science, she said, "The thing that Carl did better than anybody else I'd ever seen was this emotional connection to the sciences. He loved to tell stories . . . And when Carl talks about that on the show, we sort of made a joke that there are these things called 'Carl moments' where Carl sort of gazes dramatically off into space and the camera sort of close up, you know, close up on his face. And you can see him sort of emoting at how wonderful this is."

He's considered one of the most influential advocates for the values of science in the world because of how he expressed his passion for the subject. "When you're in love," he said, "you want to tell the world." It was this love that drove him to be a pioneer when it came to studying geology and climates on other planets. He relayed his findings in a series of popular lectures called "Planets as Places" during his time as a faculty member at Harvard University. In these lectures, Carl made another attempt to influence his students to think about worlds beyond their immediate frontier, using a combination of science and unbounded imagination. His charismatic teaching style and enthusiasm influenced people around the world.

Unlike many scientists, Carl did not want to be labeled an atheist. He was open to the possibility that science could one day find evidence of a Higher Power, even though he thought that the likelihood of that was small. He considered spirituality to be something that happened in the material world that evoked a sense of wonder.

In his book *The Demon-Haunted World: Science as a Candle in the Dark*, he wrote, "Science is not only compatible with spirituality; it is a profound source of spirituality. When we recognize our place in an immensity of light years and in the passage of ages, when we grasp the intricacy, beauty, and subtlety of life, then that soaring feeling, that sense of elation and humility combined, is surely spiritual."

After courageously fighting a rare bone marrow disease for two years, Carl took his last breath in 1996. On his passing, astrophysicist Steven Soter likened Carl to a "magnificent comet" and said, "He illuminated the lives of millions, and we will not see his like again."

During his lifetime, Carl took us to the edge of the known universe and made us all feel that we were all part of this epic, unfolding cosmic story in a way that touched the depths of mind, heart, and soul. Everyone who had been in his presence or who is now exposed to his work has the privilege of going on a celestial voyage guided by the able hands of Carl's Nomadic Soul.

In an interview with *The Cut*, his daughter Sasha Sagan said this when asked about the most valuable lessons that her parents taught her: "You are alive right this second. That is an amazing thing . . . You have the pleasure of living on a planet where you have evolved to breathe the air, drink the water, and love the warmth of the closest star. You're connected to the generations through DNA—and, even farther back, to the universe because every cell in your body was cooked in the hearts of stars. *We are star stuff.*"

Carl Sagan left an indelible legacy in science and space exploration. His work continues to remind us, and will continue to for generations to come, that if we're open and curious, "somewhere, something incredible is waiting to be known."

Understanding Our Need: The Big Questions

The History of Our Need to Believe

Since humans have inhabited the Earth, one question has confounded us: Do we live in a spiritual or material universe? The answer to this question has eluded us because we deal with unseen forces, hence the tussle between "what we see" (and can't see) and "how we look" at things.

For thousands of years, we have searched for truth and the ultimate answers to timeless questions such as:

- Who am I?
- What is my purpose?
- What is the meaning of life?

We tapped into our ingenuity to answer these eternal questions and looked around for guidance. Our brains, meaning-making machines, help us detect patterns, cause-and-effect relationships, and structures of all sorts.

Our ancestors looked to the heavens for guidance, observing the broad patterns and alignments of the stars or the omnipotence of the sun as a form of divinity we mortals could not achieve. The primitive person worshiped these heavenly bodies, for they could not fathom nor understand their origins or ages. Their enigmatic glow instilled a sense of reverie and idealism. Vincent van Gogh said, "For my part I know nothing with any certainty, but the sight of the stars makes me dream."

The propensity to dream and believe in a higher force served an evolutionary need that arose from living in times when shelter was scarce, conflicts were menacing, and predators were an immediate threat. As Scott Atran succinctly put it, "It was probably better for us to mistakenly assume that the wind was a lion than to ignore the rustling and risk death." Our search for comfort and certainty in those dark and foreboding times caused us to look up to the heavens for solace.

One of the oldest and most enduring vehicles we have used to satiate our need for spiritual curiosity is religion. In a search to understand our place in the grand scheme of things, we have attributed our being to the deities and omnipotent figures in our scriptures and mythologies. We have used these figures to develop complex notions of values, ethics, and living a fulfilling life that stretched beyond merely surviving savage predators and harsh weather. We seek enlightenment through and connection with a higher force, an entity of perfect moral standing and a bearer of infinite knowledge. Over the years, our beliefs in a Higher Power have become more structured and coded, eventually giving birth to formal religious groups that differed in their ideologies based on the era and culture each was founded in.

Eastern regions of the globe have beliefs centered on a search of insight and enlightenment, giving birth to diverse religions such as Hinduism and Buddhism. In contrast, the West pursued morality and purity to live a more fulfilling life, which evolved into religions such as Christianity and Judaism. Of course, these are just general understandings of where and how these religions developed, but they give insight into how our spiritual yearnings expressed themselves and melded with our cultures.

A 2015 Pew Research study showed that 84 percent of the world population belongs to a religion. The same study found that 90 percent of adults in the US believe in God or some form of Higher Power or spiritual force. One in five people who identify as atheists believe in some kind of higher power or spiritual force. This data attests to our evolutionary need to feel connected to something bigger than ourselves.

While philosophy, neuroscience, and anthropology cannot offer a definitive answer as to whether or not there is truth in these beliefs, what is clear is that religion has been accepted as one effective channel through which we can access meaningful connections, one that provides comfort and solace in the face of strife and uncertainty. Connecting with a Higher Power is one of our deepest human needs.

The Evolution of Faith: the Rise of Personal Spirituality

Every person has questioned where they stand in the grand scheme of things at some point in their life. We are predisposed to wonder how and why we came to be. This inquisitiveness about spirituality is a natural expression of our Nomadic Soul.

We ask whether we are born to live our days in the nine-to-five grind till our deaths or if there is a greater purpose to our existence that we are here to unlock. And we are certainly not alone in our contemplation. Many great thinkers and philosophers have argued and theorized about our place in the world. Even with excellent arguments and counterarguments, all that remains is mere speculation. Nevertheless, out of this need for understanding, countless theories and concepts have been born.

In 1859, naturalist and biologist Charles Darwin published his book *On the Origin of Species by Means of Natural Selection*, in which he theorized that we humans are no different from other creatures on the planet. This was a bold statement to make during a time when human superiority was assumed by religious institutions and the elites. He insisted that we're not divine descendants from heaven appointed to rule the planet but that we are a product of a phenomenon known as natural selection, a process through which all species of organisms evolve by inheriting genetic characteristics that increase an individual's ability to survive, compete, and procreate. Humans are a part of the survival of the fittest race along with all the other living entities on the planet.

Until the early 1500s, the reckoning of our existence in the universe was heavily influenced by religious dogma. Virtually everyone in the Western world back then believed that Earth was the center of the universe and that we humans played a prominent role in the celestial kingdom, as decreed by the church authorities. This theory was eventually challenged in 1543 by a Polish scientist named Nicolaus Copernicus, who proposed that Earth and other planets revolve around the sun. Although his model was not entirely accurate, it provided a breakthrough in the scientific world and was developed further by Galileo Galilei in 1632.

Most people and religious institutions were not ready to accept a fact that opposed their beliefs. Copernicus cleverly published his findings two months before his death to avoid being penalized for questioning the sanctity of the Catholic church's beliefs. But Galileo didn't wait until his last days to declare his findings and had to face charges for committing heresy. He found himself under house arrest.

While science has humbled us with its solid empirical evidence and theories, reminding us that we are not omnipotent beings but mere mortals trying to survive, religion and spirituality have continued to play a critical role in our way of life, helping us deal with a reality that can be unpredictable and harsh. Empires have risen and fallen. Legends have been born. Tragedies have come to pass. Throughout all of this, human existence has long been enamored with the notion of a Higher Power, and we have gone to great lengths to maintain its authority because of how it helps us cope with threats and dangers, both imminent and existential. Each day we're reminded that the line between death and survival is thin. Faith reminds us to be thankful for the gift of life.

However, in recent decades, there has been a noticeable shift in the depth of our reckoning with spirituality. According to a 2012 survey done by Adherents.com, 16 percent of the world population (approximately 1.2 billion) describes themselves to be secular or non-religious, agnostic, or atheist. Even those who are part of organized religion are becoming less involved in the practices and detached from its foundational principles.

With the growing prominence of personally defined spiritualities and secular belief systems that aren't attached to organized religions, our spiritual desires are slowly going inward. More and more people are accepting that the higher guidance they seek can be found within themselves. We can find spiritual satisfaction by upholding basic morals and aligning our actions with our purpose and values. Additionally, we can engage in activities that ground us, such as walks in nature or creative hobbies that offer an experience of transcendence.

There's an increasing number of people connecting with the transcendent through holistic modalities such as yoga, tai chi, qi gong, oracle and tarot readings, astrology, and other New Age practices. Hopping on the New Age bandwagon has become not only acceptable but popular, especially among younger generations. For many, it provides a viable alternative to the rigid structures of institutionalized religion by offering the freedom and flexibility to form their own beliefs and practices. New Age spirituality is also rooted in the ideas of self-empowerment and self-discovery, two important values to the emerging population of New Age enthusiasts.

What these trends show is that people are realizing there is no one path when it comes to connection with something bigger than ourselves. There is no right way or wrong way—just the way that is right for you. Whether you choose to meet your needs through religion, science, creative endeavors, or New Age practices, find something that best fulfills your Nomadic Soul's desire to traverse deeper dimensions. An individual spiritual practice involves finding a sense of purpose and peace. It's an inner discovery that you embark on to develop beliefs around life's meaning and connection with everything and everyone.

The State of Religion Today

While spirituality is a personalized practice that people create to access meaning, peace, and purpose, religion is a specific set of organized practices and beliefs shared by a group. As Yuval Noah Harari put it, "Religion is a deal, whereas spirituality is a journey." Each religion has different teachings and rituals, but they all reveal a spiritual dimension to life and offer ways to access spirituality through prayer and other practices.

While there are a growing number of atheists and agnostics, that does not mean that religion is irrelevant. It's estimated that 84 percent of the global population practices some type of religion. That's over 6.9 billion people. Their beliefs range from long-established faiths like Christianity to more modern spiritual traditions like Wicca.

Most people follow one of these five major religions: Christianity, Islam, Judaism, Hinduism, or Buddhism. However, each major denomination may also have completely distinct offshoots, and there are many more religions in the world.

The religious profile of the world is rapidly shifting, driven by the size of the youth population, fertility rates, and people switching belief systems. A 2015 Pew Research study shows that Christians will remain the largest religious group over the next four decades, but Islam will grow faster than any other major religion. If the current growth trend continues, Islam will catch up to Christianity by 2050. With over 4,200 estimated distinct religious belief systems, it's clear that humans have a deep need for faith.

There are many theories about why we have religion. An early view is that our hunter-gatherer ancestors needed it to foster tolerance and cooperation in their clans. This was the initial impulse that influenced our need to believe.

Over time, humans realized that religion benefited them in practical and emotional matters. Herc are seven reasons behind the human inclination for reverence and piety:

1. **To understand their place in the world.** As meaning-seeking creatures, we want to understand the different phenomena and become conscious of how and if we can impact the world around us.

2. **To feel a sense of belonging.** We are social animals with a deep need for community. Religion offers the container of safety and familiarity that we naturally crave.

3. **To create stories about cultures and history.** We have immense works of art, literature, myths, stories, and history rooted in religion. Religion, then, is an effective way to preserve heritage and culture.

4. **To receive support in daily life.** Religion can offer support when we need it, whether through the power of prayer, a community of like-minded people, or the consulting of a holy person. It comforts us as we face the perils and uncertainty of life.

5. **To find consolation in the idea of an afterlife.** The promise of an afterlife was a significant source of comfort for

people throughout history. An idyllic afterlife excited them and made it easier to endure hardships in their everyday lives.

6. To experience peace and compassion. Worship practices involve music, dance, and prayer that evoke the right-brain sensations of euphoria and transcendence. For the weary and the crestfallen, religion offers heart-opening experiences that make us feel good and boost our empathy.

7. To make sense of evil. Human beings are capable of doing evil things. Religion offers solace and redemption for those who feel that they have been wronged. Knowing that those who have committed atrocities will pay for their acts in the hereafter makes people more responsible and accountable.

The Benefits of Connecting with a Higher Power

Some skeptics view our need to have faith in a Higher Power as nothing more than a primitive coping mechanism or a New Age crutch that humans lean on to deal with the uncertainties and unpleasant realities of life. Yet cynics cannot diminish the importance of the Nomadic Souls' instinct to believe in an omnipotent form that's beyond our understanding. A Higher Power plays a crucial role in our well-being and sense of self.

It's been proven by a number of social scientists and psychologists that the absence of a belief system that resonates with us can cause us to feel empty, disconnected, and lost. This spiritual crisis has led to an increasing dependence on addictive substances commonly used to fill up the void that a person experiences when there is a lack of faith, hope, benevolence, compassion, and morality in their life.

All of us experience ups and downs in our life. It's just part of the human experience. But if we want to thrive, we need to get off the roller coaster of emotions. Without a strong foundation, we might manage temporarily until life throws us another curveball that knocks us off kilter and challenges our sense of control. But the freedom that we seek can't come from force or strategic planning alone. We need to cocreate our solutions with the energies around us. We do this by doing our part to the best of our abilities and letting go of our need to control the outcome.

When we surrender our need for control to unseen benevolent forces, we feel comforted and assured. Unsurprisingly, multiple studies have proven that people who have faith and are optimistic about the future are considerably less prone to developing mental health problems, heart disease, and stress-related conditions. On the other hand, people convinced that we lead a random and solitary existence are more likely to miss out on crucial life lessons that could lead to growth and self-actualization. Their cynicism prevents them from making meaning of significant life events critical to their Nomadic Soul's evolution.

When we believe deep in our hearts that there are things beyond our understanding, that the future is unknown, and that we may not always understand why things happen the way they do, we remain humble and more willing to accept our reality. When we see the higher purpose in our struggle, it helps us cope with pain and loss with greater faith, hope, and optimism. Though spirituality may not cure all the problems in the world, it effectively soothes our hearts and calms our minds.

Believing in a conscious universe, where everything is perfectly orchestrated and harmoniously designed, also makes sense on a practical level. Spirituality allows us to focus on the present and not be so haunted by our past mistakes or anxious about tomorrow's choices. This boosts our concentration level and our overall productivity. Whenever we hit those nefarious speed bumps, we'll be able to handle them with courage and acceptance and glean wisdom from every experience.

Another benefit of feeling connected to a higher power is that it makes us more grateful. So often we take for granted the good that happens to us, partly because our expectations are higher and partly because our anxieties for the future make our progress seem smaller than it is. When we acknowledge our progress, we propel ourselves even more. The grounding effect of spirituality allows us to see and appreciate things as they are while we hope for more.

Even though hope isn't tangible or easily measurable, experts like Jerome Groopman, who wrote *The Anatomy of Hope*, say that researchers are learning that a change in mindset has the power to alter our brain's neurochemistry. Groopman writes, "Belief and expectation—the key elements of hope—can block pain by releasing the brain's endorphins and enkephalins, mimicking the effects of morphine. In some cases, hope can also affect fundamental physiological processes like respiration, circulation, and motor function."

Hope is also a natural stress reliever, which strengthens our immune system. When we're plagued by chronic stress, our nervous system releases a flood of stress hormones, including adrenaline and cortisol, which can increase inflammation and weaken our immune system. By cultivating hope, we can free ourselves from stress, reducing our cortisol levels to restore a strong and healthy immune system.

Individuals who believe in a Higher Power are also more compassionate toward people and creatures around them. This compassion stems from understanding the interconnectedness between every living entity on the planet. Everyone and everything plays an important role in the grand scheme of things. We are all on this journey together.

Finding Connection in Non-Secular Beliefs and Philosophies

Spirituality is different for each of us. Your spirituality may not have a religious or metaphysical component but could simply involve the act of going inward. Perhaps you get your dose of spirituality from going on retreats, quiet reflection, art, or gazing at a sunset or a starry sky. We can experience a sense of transcendence, deep aliveness, and interconnectedness in many ways if we're willing to look for it. Several philosophies don't emphasize the otherworldly aspects of life but instead focus more on the rational and moral faculty. Two of them have gained popularity over the past few decades: humanism and Stoicism.

Humanism is a philosophy that focuses on secular ethics and morals without religion or a belief in a deity. It embraces human reasoning and philosophical naturalism while rejecting superstition and dogma. It was born during the Renaissance, when people began to take more interest in cultural achievements and self-actualization.

Stoics embrace the humanist approach to an ethical life but also take an interest in natural sciences, metaphysics, social science, and philosophy. Stoicism's origins date back to the third century BCE when it was founded by ancient Greek and Roman philosophers like Epictetus, Seneca, and Marcus Aurelius.

Stoicism has gained appeal in the modern age because it's compatible with the values of our time. People want to feel happier, reduce negative feelings, and build character. Stoicism offers a practical framework informed by science and reason to achieve this and live well. Its most significant appeal is its flexibility in terms of spiritual beliefs. Flexible agnosticism means that adherents can still pursue a religious path if it helps them become better human beings and live virtuously. Stoic philosopher Marcus Aurelius said, "Things are either isolated units, or they form one inseparable whole. If that whole be God, then all is well; but if aimless chance, at least you need not be aimless also."

Followers of Stoicism can have the "best of both worlds": a belief system grounded in logic, science, and morality and one that still has room for faith in a higher power. If we try, we can find the spiritual in the physical. Our time on Earth presents plenty of opportunities to grow, learn, and evolve.

Assessment: What Do You Believe?

If you're still unsure about your connection to a Higher Power, try this simple self-reflection exercise to stimulate your contemplation and thought process.

Step 1: Think of a challenging experience you've had in the past.

Step 2: Write down how you felt at the time.

Step 3: Where are you at this point in the same area of life?

Step 4: Looking back, how do you think this event contributed to your current circumstances? Do you see any obvious or subtle connections between your past and present?

Step 5: How do you make sense of the connections between the past and the present? What part did you play in those connections? What role did external influences play in those connections? Do you think higher forces influenced the outcome, or was it a product of random events (or a combination of both)?

Regardless of your perspective, pick a Higher Power or spiritual practice that inspires you to become a better person. What ultimately matters is not what we believe but how it influences our behavior and how we treat others and the environment. If your path to Higher Power leads you to become a person of character who does good in the world during your lifetime, you're on the right track.

His Holiness the 14th Dalai Lama said, "This is my simple religion. No need for temples. No need for complicated philosophy. Your own mind, your own heart is the temple. Your philosophy is simple kindness." Kindness, purpose, and altruism are essential components of the evolutionary path of a Nomadic Soul.

Digging Deep: How to Find (and Walk) Your Higher Path

How to Meet Our Need to Connect with a Higher Power

Not all of us are comfortable dealing with abstract phenomena that we can't see or comprehend. For this reason, many find it challenging to connect with a Higher Power, especially when these practices interrupt our daily routines. Others find it scary and foreboding to plummet into the depths of the unknown, while some consider it impractical and unnecessary.

In the past, religion offered answers and a gateway to the uncertainties of life. But in a world that's growing increasingly secular due to social and cultural shifts, people are gradually losing touch with the mysteries of life. Our stratospheric successes over the past century have inadvertently given us a sense of grandiosity. We don't want to be reminded of our smallness and vulnerability in a cosmic ocean that seems impersonal, random, and outside of our grasp.

However, succumbing to these fears can cause us to miss out on a significant component of the human experience. This self-assured hubris accompanied by a shallow perspective limited to life on the material plane can lead to feelings of emptiness and complacency. Our Nomadic Soul is wired to ask the big questions and consider our place in the grand scheme of things. We can train our minds to revel in the wonderment of living in a limitless universe.

By directing our focus to deeper realms of life and engaging in certain interests and hobbies, we can make contact with the higher planes of existence without feelings of discomfort and doubt. Here are three portals that can provide us direct access to that sublime force that's greater than ourselves:

Step 1: Become a student of astronomy

Astronomy has always had a significant impact on our species. Humans looked to the sky to navigate journeys and organize their lives. The knowledge we have gained from the stars ranges from when to plant our crops to understanding our origins. Early civilizations associated celestial bodies with gods and took their movements across the sky as prophecies of what was to come. When Copernicus asserted that Earth was not the center of the universe, he received a lot of resistance. His theory instigated a revolution that made religion, science, and society develop a new worldview.

To this day, astronomy opens our eyes, gives meaning to our place in the universe, and can shape our perspective on how we see the world. As our understanding of the world progresses and we unravel more mysteries, we find ourselves returning to the stories that the celestial realms tell us. Especially when we discovered that the essential elements we see in stars, such as carbon, hydrogen, oxygen, and nitrogen, are the same elements that make up our bodies, this further deepened the connection between us and the skies.

As Carl Sagan pointed out, not only is science compatible with spirituality, but it is a profound source of spirituality. Pursuing an interest in astronomy can answer fundamental questions about being human. The Greek philosopher Plato once said, "Astronomy compels the soul to look upward and leads us from this world to another." We can feel inspired to answer these questions when we develop our connection to the cosmos.

Here are some ways that you can engage more with the stars and beyond:

- **Look up at the night sky.** An easy way to instantly connect with the cosmic plane is to step out at night and look up at the starry sky. Allow yourself to get lost in the vastness and depth of space. Gaze at the planets that can be seen with the naked eye, map out the recognizable constellations, and delight in special phenomena such as eclipses, meteor showers, and comet visits. If you want a closer look, purchase a telescope to watch all the action from home. If you're in an area with hazy or cloudy skies, visit locations known to have exceptionally clear night skies, such as a desert or an ocean. It's unfathomable how big the universe is. It can be humbling when you try to probe the infinity of space and are faced with the overwhelming smallness of Earth, an insignificant celestial body lost in all the darkness.

- **Watch space-themed documentaries and movies and read books.** The skies have been a constant source of inspiration for scientists and artists alike, which is why some produced creations that we relish today. Outer space has inspired a plethora of documentaries, books, and movies. Cable channels like National Geographic and the Discovery Channel air comprehensive features on all areas of astronomy. If you like documentaries, you will enjoy special astronomy series such as Carl Sagan's *Cosmos* or *Through the Wormhole*, narrated by actor Morgan Freeman, and *Into the Universe*, by theoretical physicist and cosmologist Stephen Hawking. If you gravitate toward a story format based on a fictional narrative, you'll enjoy the splendor of the elaborate sets and CGI effects featured in movies such as *Star Wars, Star Trek, Interstellar, Martian,* and *Apollo 13*, to name a few. There are picture books and encyclopedias with high-quality images of space for both children and adults. You can find plenty of pictures and features on the internet and social media and follow space-oriented organizations such as NASA or astronomy influencers such as Neil deGrasse Tyson.

- **Visit planetariums, science museums, and space stations.** Have a more immersive experience of space exploration by visiting planetariums, science museums, and space stations around the world. Each venue has features such as exhibits, documentaries, observatories, tours, and narrators who provide in-depth knowledge about various space phenomena, including the human history of space travel. Let yourself get lost in places such as The Smithsonian's National Air and Space Museum in Washington, DC, the Kennedy Space Center in Central Florida, the Science Museum in London, and the Hong Kong Space Museum, to name a few. Allocate plenty of time on your visit to soak in material and study the exhibits.

Step 2: Explore different spiritual and religious paths

Spirituality is different for each of us. It's a broad concept that can include many beliefs and philosophies. For you, spirituality may center around the faith you grew up in, like Christianity, Islam, Judaism, Hinduism, or Buddhism. Being part of your community and reading the scriptures might invoke the sacred within you. Alternatively, your spirituality may not have a religious component but could simply involve the act of introspection. Here are some ways to broaden your knowledge base when it comes to different spiritual and religious paths:

- **Expose yourself to the works of mystics and religions.** Besides engaging in space exploration, there are other paths you can take to experience transcendence. These pathways originate from the copious collections of folklore, stories, and practices accumulated throughout human history. We can learn about these different paths by reading about the experiences of those who had direct experiences of connecting to deeper realms of existence. Look into reading the works of mystics such as Saint Teresa of Avila, Thomas Merton, and Kahlil Gibran. If you're open to it, read religious scriptures, take a class on world religions, or watch a documentary series such as Oprah's *Belief* to get an overview of the basics of various faiths.

- **Respect all faiths and belief systems.** As you learn about different points of view on divinity, approach everything from a place of openness. Tap into the natural curiosity of your Nomadic Soul to discern the perspectives and guiding principles of each path. You don't have to agree with whatever you come across in your exploration, but avoid judging or labeling what you find out as good or bad. If you sense that you're slipping into a critical frame of mind, do your best to return to neutrality. Remember that everyone has the right to choose their own belief systems. Throughout history, humanity's inability to live peacefully with people of other faiths has led to too many wars, deaths, and meaningless acts of crime. We can break that vicious cycle by demonstrating tolerance and a willingness to live in a society where everyone is allowed to follow their chosen faiths, because we know that diversity in thought and beliefs is what makes our planet a beautiful place.

- **Visit spiritual and religious sites.** Since ancient times, people have considered travel a passage to divine inspiration and elevated states of being. Sacred journeys, known as pilgrimages, are taken to shrines and places of significance. Examples include the Camino de Santiago in Spain, the Golden Temple in Amritsar, Mecca in Saudi Arabia, the Sistine Chapel in Vatican City, and Machu Picchu in Peru. These locations are considered sacred to devotees because of their spiritual importance. They are places where a deity is believed to reside, that resonate with otherworldly powers, where miracles have been witnessed, or where a founder or saint was born, passed away, or had their spiritual awakening. Pilgrims embark on these sacred journeys to be healed, have questions answered, or receive blessings. Visiting these sites might give us access to mystical experiences and the high-vibration energy believed to permeate these hallowed grounds.

- **Develop your own beliefs and practices.** Some people choose to stick with the faith and religious doctrines they grew up with, while others develop their own independent views based on their inclinations, education, and life experience. Whichever path you choose, develop a clear framework for what you believe in, as well as the values, ethics, rituals, practices, and virtues you express. In his book *A Religion of One's Own*, former monk and psychotherapist Thomas Moore said, "I want to promote a religion that is felt and not just thought out, meaningful and not just emotional, my own and not just an ancient tradition." Moore understands the disillusionment of the millions of people in our modern era who do not relate to the inflexible teachings of formal religion. Many have abandoned it altogether and live unsatisfying and empty lives because of the lack of a spiritual path. In his book, Moore suggests a middle way where we draw elements from a variety of spiritual traditions so that we can infuse our lives with transcendence. He wrote, "The point is not to join the right group, but to find resources that will take you deep into your search and give you penetrating insights. Wisdom does not lose value because it lacks the correct institutional affiliation."

  While immersing yourself in your studies of other religious and spiritual traditions, you'll pick up on values, morals, and principles to guide you on your path. Although all religions promote a framework centered on morality, generosity, kindness, and self-awareness, perhaps you connect deeper with the narratives, imagery, and practices of one or more paths over the others.

You might resonate with the deities from Greek polytheism or the mindfulness practices of Buddhism and the shamanic rituals of Native American traditions all at the same time. You have the freedom to create your own routines and rituals based on your beliefs, which ground you with love, faith, peace, and comfort. This may include prayer, chanting, specific ceremonies, dancing, reading scripture, and countless others. If you're someone who has chosen a secular perspective, your best path to experiencing the sublime and a sense of wonder is through studying astronomy and science and connecting with the natural world. You can look to philosophies such as Stoicism, which have existed since the days of ancient Greece and have guided some of the greatest leaders in history, such as President Theodore Roosevelt and Marcus Aurelius.

Step 3: Step away from the mundane

Have you ever asked yourself, "Is this all there is?" Stuck on the treadmill of life, you may have tried to find meaning in the mundane. If life is starting to feel gray, colorless, and monotonous, that is a nudge from your Nomadic Soul reminding you that you're not meant to live like a robot. You have a vivid imagination, a creative inclination, and a need for novelty and vibrancy. Take time from your daily routine to enter the realm of wonder and transcendence.

Here are some ways you can experience deeper dimensions of being in the world:

- **Go off the beaten track.** Sometimes, stepping out and getting away from the environment where we spend most of our time is all it takes to shake things up and put us in a different frame of mind. Take a break from your routine and visit natural sites in your city or other parts of the world. The more remote and distant we are from civilization, the more sacred and unique our experience will be. Some examples of places like this are towns, cities, and countries with vastly different cultures or locales and magnificent landscapes such as a large expanse of snow or water or a big mountain or cliff. When we encounter such places, we're reminded that we are not the center of everything and that there's so much more to life than the concerns and minutiae of everyday life.

- **Visit historical and archeological museums**. Seeing artifacts created by humans from thousands of years ago or even seeing their remains can instantly connect you with the human thread of life and fill you with feelings of timelessness. As you wander around the museum, soak in all the beauty and magnificence of each piece, imagining the dedication, effort, and devotion that went into making a particular painting, sculpture, pottery, utensil, etc. Whether it is the mysterious gaze of the *Mona Lisa*, a piece of an archway from a majestic Greek temple, or an incredibly well-preserved Egyptian mummy, each artifact tells a story of the people who made it. It gives us a strong sense of the values, hopes, and fears that define the artist's belief system. Even though the people who created them are long gone, they left behind a legacy that lived on much longer than they could have possibly imagined. Each era, dynasty, and civilization had thousands of stories, each one contributing to the one big story of the human life form. You can't help but be in awe when you think about the thousands of events that had to converge for life to flourish on Earth.

- **Engage in art.** Another powerful medium where we can experience a sense of timelessness is creativity. Any form of artistic expression will give us access to the mystic ethers through which inspiration flows. Seeking an outlet to channel our most profound ideas is a powerful way to give form to the unconscious intelligence that lies within us. Seasoned creative professionals such as artists, musicians, dancers, and writers will tell you how they can access flow and a higher plane of inspiration while working on their craft. Michael Jackson captured the sublime nature of this state when he said, "People ask me how I make music. I tell them I just stepped into it. It's like stepping into a river and joining the flow. Every moment in the river has its song."

  Experiences of artists like Michael Jackson attest to the power of art and how it can open a portal to the deeper and sacred part of our being. Our creations are nothing but a direct expression of our soul essence. The good news is that we don't have to be in a traditional creative career to enter deeper dimensions of flow. We can always take up a hobby such as painting, dancing, or singing, among many others, to experience the same benefits. We can also consume different forms of art to experience this sentiment. Whether that includes being captivated by the mesmerizing melodies of a song or the evocative storyline of a play or the dance routine of a maestro, we benefit just as much as the patron and the artist.

See the Extraordinary in the Ordinary

When you're aligned with a higher consciousness that goes beyond the superficial and physical, you'll find the extraordinary in the ordinary. You'll see wonder in the simplest things, like a rosebud or a person's smile. You gain a heightened sensitivity to beauty and are more connected to the oneness of all things. Whether it's the touch of a baby's hand, the rhythmic ripples you feel in your body after a gong is struck, or the scent of a freshly baked apple pie that floods you with memories of your grandmother, you start to find joy in the tableau of daily life. Through this lens of wonder, a whole new world will reveal itself to you.

But the path of the Nomadic Soul is not sprinkled with fairy dust. As demonstrated in the stories of the six inspirational figures in previous chapters, it requires brutal self-honesty and facing hardships with grace and resilience. You'll have to deal with your fault lines while also developing the ability to notice signs, synchronicities, and opportunities for your evolution and growth. But if you say "yes" to this journey, you'll wake up from a dream of everyday, material-level, ego-based reality to a higher spirit-based consciousness.

It's not that you won't face challenges anymore but that you will start to understand their greater purpose in the grand scheme of things, making it easier to flow and adjust. You will begin to trust that a higher plan is at play and that you are a cocreator in its unfolding. You will develop a deeper understanding of yourself and your connection to others and the universe. You will start to see the extraordinary in the ordinariness of your life, no matter what's happening to you, because you search for it.

By learning how to live consciously, treating everything and everyone with reverence, you train yourself to add dimension and depth to every moment you have. You savor your experiences and appreciate your good fortune and the lessons. You realize that we're living in a universe where everything that occurs, good and bad, can be used to transform us. As you evolve your belief in the unknowable and unseeable, you move closer to your boundless potential as a Nomadic Soul. After all, nearly all the elements in your body were made in a star.

"We are made of star stuff," as Carl Sagan said. "We are a way for the cosmos to know itself."

Conclusion

The Path to an Eternal Life

"And you? When will you begin
that long journey into yourself?"—Rumi

People who are aligned with their Nomadic Soul are deeply aware that someday their journey on Earth will come to an end. Yet this profound knowing of the inevitable end does not dishearten them. Instead, it emboldens them to get the most out of every moment in their life.

Like a shooting star that blazes across the sky, we briefly pass through this celestial frontier to experience life on planet Earth. We exist for a short stint in cosmic time. Our home is a minuscule pale-blue planet—an isolated speck of stardust obscured in the unfathomably vast darkness of space. Millions have visited before us, and there will most likely be many more to follow when we bid adieu. Life will go on.

When seen from this perspective, it's easy to become skeptical about our place in the grander scheme of things. A cynic might wonder, "What's the point? We're all going to perish one day, so why not just live for fun and frivolity and stay in the familiar realm of the physical plane? Time is limited, so why waste it on deep thought and plunging into the depths of our being?" At first glance, these are perfectly valid questions that should be taken seriously.

There's nothing inherently wrong with living an unexamined, shallow life. In fact, many people choose to live on the periphery of a soulful existence, opting for a lifestyle of accumulating material riches, status, and power. Many people in this position succeed in their endeavors and seem happy and prosperous on the surface. However, there will always be a part of them that will feel like something is missing in their life. Without a consciously built soul compass, they lack direction, depth, and purpose.

A dull ache of apathy pulsates through every fiber of their being. They will attempt to assuage their dissatisfaction through escapism, "toys," and self-medication. By ignoring the call for inner liberation from their Nomadic Soul, they get stuck in the murky and dark realm of ego and fear. There are countless examples of wealthy and famous people who were ensnared by the trappings of success. Material abundance took them to unprecedented heights of prosperity, but they failed to anchor themselves in meaningful endeavors and a set of ethics and morals. They forgot what really matters at the end of the day. No designer shoes, fancy car, or trophy spouse can ever substitute for a soul that's been nurtured. Sadly, many of them realize this too late.

In the superficial domain ruled by materialism and ego, it's almost impossible to capture the kaleidoscopic beauty and wonder that come from living a wholehearted existence. Only through the way of the Nomadic Soul can we dare to dream big and set forth on adventures that will lead to blossoming of our capacity.

Our aim should not be perfection. We're all at different evolutionary stages of awakening our Nomadic Soul, and the process looks different for everyone. It's not linear and predictable but filled with twists, turns, and unpredictable events that can benefit or challenge us. At one stage, we might take one step forward and, at another, two steps back. You might be a master at meeting your need for creative expression but a novice at meeting your need for connection. That's why we need to be patient and have compassion for ourselves and trust our inner compass as we walk our journey. It is okay to awaken at our own pace, in our own way. There are no rights and wrongs, just what feels suitable for you and your circumstances.

The awakening process has been seen in various religions worldwide, and it goes by different names, such as *enlightenment* or *nirvana*. No matter what it's called, soul awakening describes the process of gaining the awareness that there is more to life than living on autopilot. There are deeper layers meant to be explored during our time on Earth. The path of the Nomadic Soul prompts us to ask existential questions like, "Why am I here?" and "Who am I?" It can be unnerving and bring up angst and concern, but it can also elicit excitement and awe, depending on the catalyst for the awakening. It gives us a new sense of being in the world, and there's no going back to the old ways.

As you develop a relationship with the sacred dimensions of life, you can see that you are never alone but are one small part of an interconnected whole. Through this process, your consciousness grows, often accompanied by the desire to transform yourself to create change in the world. After you've spent time searching and doing the internal work, you'll develop enough self-awareness to give up aspects of yourself that are not part of your true nature. You may lose your ego identity or your subjective self and experience a sense of oneness with the universe. This ego-death has been called moksha and bodhi (enlightenment) in Eastern traditions. As you let go of anything that no longer aligns with your soul's highest expression, you come home to your Nomadic Soul—the part of you that defines your soul essence. You develop faith in the unknown and know you are cocreating your future with the universe.

When we follow the footsteps of our inner seer, we can embrace and follow through with our soul's purpose, lessons, and what we're here to achieve during our lifetime. We know that there is a reason for us being here and that we play a crucial role in this thriving ecosystem. Just as we need honeybees to pollinate the flowers, trees to give us oxygen, and animals to provide us with love and nourishment, we are here to accomplish something profound and impactful, which can only be done by us. Our mission is to find out what that is as early as possible in life and get moving in that direction. The sooner we start, the more time we can devote to finding our stride until we strike gold.

Once you internalize the significance and enormity of your being alive on this planet in this day and age, you'll appreciate that your life is precious. The world needs you to show up and express your gifts. Your guide to the unfolding of your magnificence is your Nomadic Soul. Prioritizing your life around fulfilling its needs will ensure that you stay true to your unique mission.

When you understand your reason for being here, not only will you transform into a person of substance and character, but you'll also strengthen your capacity to make the world a better place—because the Nomadic Soul ultimately seeks to love and enhance the lives of others. When living in this elevated state of being, you'll see that life is ultimately about the giving and receiving of energies. We're all here to contribute to the world and leave behind a legacy from which future generations can reap the rewards. Your legacy could be your children, who will grow up to be kind and responsible citizens, or it could be all the people you touch with your creative gifts and talents. The scale and reach don't matter. What matters is the heart and effort that you put into materializing your intentions.

With love and charity as your guideposts, you'll insulate yourself from false illusions and the facades erected by a society predominantly entranced by ego-based desires. You'll opt to weave your legacy with threads of enlightenment, humility, and self-actualization. It is the metaphorical Yellow Brick Road journey that will lead you toward freedom and connection. This road will lead you back to your true home—the sacred abode of your Nomadic Soul.

True power is, and always will be, within you.

Acknowledgments

The seeds of this book were planted many years ago when my parents took me on their travels around the world. We visited museums, natural wonders, sacred sites, amusement parks, and bustling cities. All these experiences broadened my horizons and trained me to see the sublime in the mundane and to find something special in everyone I met.

My father encouraged me to watch educational shows, read the works of the greats, and explore vistas beyond what I could see. My mother impressed upon me the importance of hard work, discipline, and humility. I'm immensely indebted to both for opening the doorways of my mind, heart, and soul and for giving me the resources to harness and develop my strengths.

I also want to thank Oprah Winfrey, whose conversations started me on the self-improvement path as a young adult. Reading the works of her show's guests—Dr. Wayne Dyer, Dr. Phil McGraw, Cheryl Richardson, Martha Beck, and Gary Zukav—changed my life and who I was on a fundamental level. So, thank you, Oprah, for being a pioneer and using your platform to create a paradigm shift in my life and the world.

The Nomadic Soul is also a product of magic. As a lover of this art form, I see magic as a metaphor for the power of the mind. It's about achieving the impossible and making the invisible visible. It reminds us that the power of manifestation lies within us if we're willing to search for it. Artists such as Walt Disney and performers such as David Copperfield made me believe in magic and wonder—and for that, I'm grateful.

To all my mentors, teachers, therapists, and coaches, your words and guidance made me a strong and confident person, healed my wounds, and spurred me to use my voice and talents to contribute something meaningful to society.

Lastly, I want to give special thanks to my agent, Steve Harris, who believed in me and my message, and to the team at Amplify Publishing for helping me realize my vision.

About the Author

Seline Shenoy is an author, blogger, and podcaster whose work focuses on personal development, self-esteem, productivity, and culture. After working as a life and career coach for six years, Seline founded The Dream Catcher, a digital community that encourages its members to live their authentic dream life and make a difference in the world. Seline is the primary writer for The Dream Catcher, which has been sharing its inspirational message with thousands of monthly readers across the world since 2014.

In 2018, she launched *The Dream Catcher* podcast, which features candid conversations with over one hundred and fifty self-help and spiritual wellness experts, including bestselling authors, influencers, spiritual leaders, and scholars. She is the author of *Beauty Redefined: How to Feel Authentically Beautiful in Today's World* (Austin Macauley Publishers, 2018), a guide to finding and redefining beauty standards.

In addition to her work on The Dream Catcher and *The Dream Catcher* podcast, Seline is a content creator, copywriter, and branding strategist. Over the past fifteen years, she's been a part of award-winning agencies and companies in four different countries.

She's written for publications including *Forbes*, MindBodyGreen, Elite Daily, and many more. In 2021, Seline was awarded the prestigious UAE Golden Visa, a long-term residence visa granted by the Dubai Culture and Arts Authority in recognition of her contributions to writing and podcasting.

Born and raised in Dubai and educated in the United States, Seline considers herself a global citizen, having traveled to over thirty-five countries across Europe, North America, Australia, Asia, the Middle East, and Africa. Her travels inspired her mission to spread awareness about cultural and racial identity and acceptance.

Learn more about Seline and subscribe to *The Dream Catcher* podcast at SelineShenoy.com. Get free content and resources at TheDreamCatch.com.

Also by Seline Shenoy

Beauty Redefined:
How to Feel Authentically Beautiful in Today's World

In today's 24/7, never-unplugged culture, women have a world of opportunity at their fingertips. But with social media also at their fingertips, the pressure to appear flawless is at an all-time high. Despite recent movements emphasizing body positivity, research continues to show that most women are still unhappy with the way they look.

Seline Shenoy is challenging this quest for perfection with her groundbreaking new book, *Beauty Redefined: How to Feel Authentically Beautiful in Today's World* (Austin Macauley Publishers, May 31, 2018)—the antithesis of diet and fitness books that promise to help you craft the body of your dreams. Offering women the inspiration they need to become the best version of themselves, Seline reveals essential strategies to cultivate their unique talents and skills—whatever their size, shape, or background. By exposing the cultural, biological, and psychological influencers that shape our views on feminine beauty, *Beauty Redefined* ignites a much-needed revolution.

Instead of sugar-coating reality, Seline acknowledges that a woman's looks matter in today's world; however, she challenges women to discover their inner strengths, share them with the world, and create a paradigm shift that defines beauty by character instead of appearance. The tricky road to self-love is filled with emotional minefields. That's why women are in dire need of guidance and tools to discover genuine self-acceptance. This book is for the woman who is ready to overcome self-doubt and initiate positive change so she can embody a wholehearted and conscious way of living.

Download a free book chapter and "The True Beauty Manifesto" at BeautyRedefinedBook.com.

"All in all, Beauty Redefined *is more than just a beauty book. It was part history, part self-help, part social manifesto. I enjoyed it a lot, and I think it's something that a lot of women who struggle with self-esteem issues could get a lot out of."*

– Pamela, book reviewer on goodreads.com